PICTORIAL HISTORY OF THE
US 3RD ARMORED DIVISION
IN WORLD WAR TWO

Pictorial History of the US 3rd Armored Division in World War Two

Darren Neely

Pen & Sword
MILITARY

First published in Great Britain in 2020 by
Pen & Sword Military
An imprint of
Pen & Sword Books Ltd
Yorkshire – Philadelphia

ISBN 978 1 52677 551 1

Typeset by Mac Style
Printed and bound by CPI Group (UK) Ltd, Croydon, CR0 4YY

Pen & Sword Books Limited incorporates the imprints of Atlas,
Archaeology, Aviation, Discovery, Family History, Fiction, History,
Maritime, Military, Military Classics, Politics, Select, Transport, True
Crime, Air World, Frontline Publishing, Leo Cooper, Remember
When, Seaforth Publishing, The Praetorian Press, Wharncliffe Local
History, Wharncliffe Transport, Wharncliffe True Crime and White
Owl.

For a complete list of Pen & Sword titles please contact

PEN & SWORD BOOKS LIMITED
47 Church Street, Barnsley, South Yorkshire, S70 2AS, England
E-mail: enquiries@pen-and-sword.co.uk
Website: www.pen-and-sword.co.uk

Or

PEN AND SWORD BOOKS
1950 Lawrence Rd, Havertown, PA 19083, USA
E-mail: Uspen-and-sword@casematepublishers.com
Website: www.penandswordbooks.com

CONTENTS

Introduction   vi

Chapter 1   1

Chapter 2   74

Chapter 3   149

Chapter 4   225

INTRODUCTION

During the European Theater of Operations (ETO) in the Second World War, the 3rd Armored Division of the US Army was one of, if not the finest, fighting units fielded by the American Army. The 3rd Armored, known as 'Spearhead' fought in almost every major engagement in the ETO except for the Normandy invasion landings and was constantly at the forefront of the advance of the American and Allied armies as they made their way from France and to the River Elbe of Germany in 1945. The 3rd Armored along with the 2nd Armored were the only armored divisions that were formed under the 'heavy' designation, meaning they had two complete armored regiments with three tank battalions each and an armored infantry regiment, whereas the other standard American armored divisions comprised three tank and three armored infantry battalions each.

In addition to the two armored regiments (32nd and 33rd) and one armored infantry regiment (36th), the division also had three armored field artillery battalions (54th, 67th, 391st), a tank destroyer battalion (703rd), an armored reconnaissance battalion (83rd), an armored engineer battalion (23rd), a medical battalion (45th), an anti-aircraft battalion (486th) and battalion-sized supply and ordnance/maintenance units. The division was typically broken down into two Combat Commands (CCA and CCB) that were centered on the two armored regiments and complemented by armored infantry, artillery, engineers, etc. There was also a smaller combat command, CCR, which was used as a reserve unit when needed.

The 3rd Armored would land on the Normandy beaches in the Omaha Beach sector in mid-June 1944 and make their way to the front lines shortly after. The commander of the division was Major General Leroy H. Watson. The 3rd Armored would soon receive their baptism of fire at Villiers-Fossard on June 29/30 1944 when units of CCA would assist the 29th Infantry Division in straightening the front lines. The tank units of the 32nd Armored Regiment would receive a bloody nose in these initial engagements and quickly come to realize how effective the German anti-tank defenses in the Normandy hedgerows were. By the second week of July the entire division was engaged with the enemy at the front lines and French locations like Haut Vents, Vire, Pont-Hébert and Saint Lo became all too familiar names for the men of Spearhead. In early

August, Major General Watson was replaced on the orders of the VII Corps commander Major General Joe Collins, who felt a change was needed. Major General Maurice Rose would assume command and lead the division until his tragic death at the hands of a German tank commander on March 30 1945 near Paderborn, Germany. General Rose was a dynamic commander who had the respect of his men and superiors and was frequently found near the front lines with his troops.

After a brief break to learn from their initial Normandy engagements, including fitting their tanks with steel devices to break through the hedgerows, the 3rd Armored was prepared to lead the Allied efforts to close their end of the Falaise Pocket in August 1944. The 3rd Armored smashed German panzer divisions as they advanced rapidly across France. Fierce battles raged in places like Ranes, Fromental and Mortain as the 3rd Armored began to master tank warfare in the Normandy countryside. By the end of August, the 3rd Armored had completed its sweep across France and was knocking on the door of occupied Belgium. The advance through Belgium was met with cheerful Belgian crowds as they inscribed graffiti on the American tanks as they made their way through the small towns and cities of Belgium.

However, it was here in September 1944 at the Westwall or Siegfried Line of Germany and the area around Stolberg where the 3rd Armored would spend the remainder of 1944 before shifting to the Ardennes to counter the German offensive known as the Battle of the Bulge. A combination of a spirited German defense, weather and quagmires in other sectors near the 3rd Armored resulted in a grueling stalemate in this sector for the American First Army which VII Corps and the 3rd Armored were part of. Towns like Stolberg, Mausbach, Hastenrath, Werth, Geich and Langerwehe are where the 3rd Armored fought a series of slugfests with the German Army in the fall of 1944.

The German counter-offensive in the Ardennes on December 16 1944 resulted in the 3rd Armored Division being sent to the Ardennes of Belgium to assist the VII Corps in first stemming the German advance and then going on the offensive to push the Germans back to their homeland. Defeating crack German SS Panzer Divisions at places like La Gleize, Lierneux, Sterpigny, Ottre and Lomre saw heavy casualties in men and vehicles on both sides, but by the middle of January 1945, the Germans had been soundly defeated and pushed back across their border.

After a few weeks of rest and refitting, including being equipped with ten of the new M26 Pershing tanks, the 3rd Armored was ready for the final push across Germany to end the war. Spearheading across Germany quickly ensued and the first large German city on the Rhine, Cologne, fell on March 6 1945. It was here that the 3rd Armored would again gain notoriety with the famous Pershing versus Panther duel at Cologne Cathedral. (Note to readers: if you haven't read

Spearhead by Adam Makos yet, please do yourself a favor and do so immediately for an in-depth look at the life of a 3rd Armored Division tanker and also the famous tank duel at Cologne Cathedral.) Soon the 3rd Armored would be off to assist in their part of closing the Ruhr Pocket which, after General Rose's death on March 30 1945 near Paderborn, would be known as the 'Rose Pocket'. After the closing of the pocket the 3rd Armored would continue its lightning advance against spirited last-ditch resistance in small German towns in the Harz region before taking the city of Dessau and liberating Nordhausen concentration camp in late April of 1945. It was near here on the western side of the River Elbe that Spearhead ended its advance and would celebrate the end of the war in Europe in May 1945.

There has been a tremendous amount of information published about the 3rd Armored Division, in particular the battles they fought: Normandy, the Westwall, the Ardennes, Cologne and against the SS units at Paderborn. This book is not a tactical or historical review of the unit in the action against Germany in the ETO. Rather it is an attempt to show the history of the 3rd Armored through high-quality photographs. Many of these photographs have been seen before, but not as in the following format. They have been shown piecemeal and/or to supplement a tactical history. This book will show the history of the division from their arrival in Normandy to the end of the war in Germany in May 1945. These photos of the men, their weapons, equipment and vehicles are presented in chronological order and the reader can see changes in the unit as they adapted to the war in the ETO. Changes such as extra armor added to the front of tanks, logs added to the sides to help with muddy roads, and hedgerow cutters will be seen in these photos. In addition to photos of the men and equipment of the 3rd Armored Division, included here are photos of their enemy and their vaunted armor vehicles, the German Panzer. The photographs are broken down into four sections: Normandy, Westwall Stalemate, Ardennes and Spearhead across Germany. Each section will have a brief historical setting and then each photo will be presented with a caption to highlight the subject of each one.

The majority of these photographs are from the official US Army cameramen attached to the 3rd Armored during the war. The author was lucky to have direct access to photographs some of these men brought home with them after the war. Cameramen such as Joe DeMarco, W.B. Allen and Harold Roberts covered the 3rd Armored Division during the entirety of the war, and their photos are included here. Unless otherwise noted, all photographs are official US Army Signal Corps photos from the National Archives and Records Administration (NARA).

Huge thanks to the families of the above-mentioned cameramen, Joe and Rick DeMarco, Dave and Geri Allen and Joshua Roberts. An additional thanks to the staff at the 3rd Armored Division archives at the University of Illinois, the staff at the Still Pictures Branch at NARA, especially Holly Reed and staff at the archives at Stanford University. Also I would be remiss not to thank my wife Debbie and children Annie and Aidan for their patience as I assembled these photos and wrote this book. Also, my thanks to Lee Archer for the use of his photos of the 67th Armored Field Artillery Battalion and to the family of George H. Bloth for the use of his private photographs.

Darren Neely
Annapolis, MD
December 2019

CHAPTER ONE

The 3rd Armored Division had been honing their craft and training Stateside since 1942 and in England since early 1944. They were ready and eager to join the fight in Europe after the Normandy invasion on 6 June 1944. The majority of the 3rd Armored Division landed at Omaha Beach in Normandy starting on 23 June, with the remainder of the supporting units in the subsequent days. Most vehicles were able to disembark from their LSTs (Landing Ships, Tank) in dry conditions on Omaha, but some did have to deal with the surf and waves.

The division would not have to wait long for their baptism of fire in the Normandy countryside. In late June, there was an enemy salient protruding about 3,000 yards in the zone of the American 29th Infantry Division around the town of Villiers-Fossard just east of the River Vire. Combat Command A (CCA) of the 3rd Armored was given the assignment to eliminate the bulge in the lines and seize and hold Villiers-Fossard until relieved by the 29th Infantry Division. The three task forces that made up CCA from the 32nd Armored Regiment were X, Y and Z, naturally built around the three tank battalions, supporting armored infantry, tank destroyers and engineers. The attack was slated to commence on 29 June. The 3rd Armored found the area well-defended by the German 353rd Infantry Division who were firmly entrenched in the natural defenses of the hedgerow country and skillfully utilized artillery and anti-tank weapons. To assist with the hedgerows, the division was assigned some bulldozer tanks. However, this initial engagement with the enemy would prove costly and give the men of the Spearhead a bloody nose. The battle raged for two days before the bulge in the lines could be eliminated and the town taken. Tank losses were extremely high for such a short engagement: more than thirty were damaged, most being able to be repaired by the maintenance units. Approximately 100 men were killed in action, with the number of wounded close to 300. The division learned what it was like to face intense small-arms fire, anti-tank weapons and mortar barrages from a well-concealed enemy. They learned that panzerfaust and bazooka teams could cause havoc in a short period of time.

After the battles at Villiers-Fossard, the 32nd Armored Regiment was in a rest and refit mode while the 33rd Armored Regiment and other division units were brought together for their piece of action in early July. CCB, of which the 33rd Armored Regiment was the primary combat unit, was teamed with the 30th Infantry Division for an attack toward St. Gilles on 9 July. At the same time, CCA was to protect the right flank and was teamed with the 9th Infantry Division on 10 July. On 11 July, CCA was forced to move to St. Jean de Daye/Le Desert area to stem a counter- attack by the German Panzer Lehr Division. Meanwhile, CCB had its hands full on Hill 91 or Les Hauts Vents. Colonel Dorrance Roysden led a task force up the hill on 10 July with heavy losses, only to be driven off on the 11th but then the armored task force retook it and was finally relieved by the 30th Infantry Division on 16 July. The fighting in the areas of both combat commands of the 3rd Armored was intense and the counter-attack by the Panzer Lehr resulted in high tank losses for both sides. Areas with the names of Les Haut Vents, Pont-Hébert and Belle Lande would become cemented in the memories of the men of the Spearhead. In particular at Pont-Hébert, the 3rd Battalion of the 33rd Armored Regiment would lose all their command tanks, including that of Lieutenant Colonel Sam Hogan. The division learned the importance of teaming with their fellow infantry divisions and this would be critical not only in Normandy but for the duration of the war. CCA worked with the 9th Infantry Division at this time, while CCB was teamed with the 30th Infantry Division.

After these brief but intense engagements, the 3rd Armored was given about ten days to rest and refit before Operation COBRA would begin on 26 July. Replacements were brought up to the front lines, and vehicles were repaired. To assist with the continued hedgerow problem and the upcoming offensive, the 3rd Armored Division tanks were fitted with a hedgerow-cutting device called the T2 Douglas. The tank units took this time of rest to equip their tanks with this new device. On 26 July, the weather broke and the bombardment to open Operation COBRA began with the main focal point in the middle of the American VII Corps sector, of which the 3rd Armored was part between Marigny and St. Gilles. The 3rd Armored's familiar friends the 9th and 30th Infantry divisions would be involved as well, in addition to the 1st Infantry Division with which CCB would attack toward Coutances. After the Army Air Corps had done their damage, CCA would move out towards Roncey. Intense rapid movement was the name of the game with fierce engagements with German armor along the way in places like Cerisy-la-Salle, Marigny, Juvigny-le-Tertre, Villedieu-les-Poêles and Reffuveille. In addition to working with attached infantry units, the 3rd Armored began to perfect the land-air coordination with fighter-bomber units and the forward observers attached to the tank units. Air strikes were called in within minutes of engaging German armor and their results were fantastic.

The success of Operation COBRA caused extreme panic in the German high command and a doomed counter-offensive was called for around the Mortain area for 7 August, code-named Operation LÜTTICH. The German counter-attack hit smack in the middle of the 30th Infantry Division around Mortain. CCB was resting west of Reffuveille and was ordered to meet this German attack at Le Mesnil-Tôve and Le Mesnil-Adelée. The action was fierce and losses were high on both sides, but the German tank units were driven back. By 12 August the German counter-attack had sputtered. Task Force Hogan in the 33rd Armored Regiment had lost twenty-three tanks over a period of a few days. It was during this time that the 12th Army Group leadership felt a change was needed in the 3rd Armored Division and Major General Leroy Watson was replaced by Major General Maurice Rose who had been serving with the 2nd Armored Division.

With the German failed counter-attack having been dealt with and a brief rest and equipment maintenance period, the division was ready to continue the offensive and close what was now being called the Falaise Pocket. CCA moved towards Ranes and Fromental via Pré-en-Pail and Carrouges. The battles around Ranes and Fromental would once again be intense against retreating German armored forces, this time crack Waffen SS units. To further the difficulty, the men of CCA had to endure a few friendly bombing incidents at the same time. CCB was brought up from the west to help deal with the problem at Ranes and Fromental and the area was finally cleared on 17 August. CCB moved from the area around Putanges and helped seal the Falaise Pocket on 18 August when Sergeant Donald Ekdahl of the 33rd Armored Regiment shook hands with a British solder at Brest, formally closing the gap.

With the gap closed and the German armies in France and Belgium in full retreat, the attention was now turned to liberating Paris and the move towards Belgium and eventually the Westwall of Germany. The advance across Northern France into Belgium would be one of extreme rapidity as tank country was finally encountered now that the hedgerows were behind the men. The fields where many of their ancestors fought in the First World War were far more conducive to rapid tank movement than the Normandy countryside. The 3rd Armored was now in the enemy's rear communications and supply zone as the race was one for the Westwall.

The River Seine was crossed on 25 August over an existing bridge and the division was followed by men of the 1st and 9th Infantry divisions. Then just two days later the division crossed the River Marne and captured Meaux. The German army was completely disorganized and in full retreat. The only thing slowing the 3rd Armored tankers down was the mass of jubilant French and Belgian crowds they would begin to encounter as towns were liberated daily. An interesting event occurred on 29 August when two German trains were stopped near Braine, France by units of the 54th Armored Field Artillery Battalion, the 32nd Armored Regiment and the 486th AAA Battalion. One train had four

German Tiger 1 tanks on it that were being sent back for repairs and when found by the American units, a few of the tanks attempted to engage the Americans but the train was stopped and the tanks were quickly put out of action by the 3rd Armored units. The other train nearby had a Panzer IV tank on one of its transport cars, while the other cars were loaded with luxury items such as women's perfume, lingerie and other items the Germans felt necessary to send back to the homeland during the retreat. Photographs of the actions around both trains are included in the sections that follow.

On 28 August, the River Aisne was crossed and with the 83rd Armored Reconnaissance Battalion leading the way, the 3rd Armored headed into Belgium. Mons became the latest objective through Hirson and Vervins. By 1 September, six separate armored columns of the division split evenly between the three combat commands headed towards Mons and crossed the Belgian border on 2 September. In taking Mons, the 3rd Armored bagged more than 8,000 German prisoners as elated Belgian civilians looked on at their new liberators. Not taking time to enjoy the celebrations, the 3rd Armored advance units continued their advance to the Siegfried Line. On 4 September, CCB then took Namur and CCA moved past Charleroi. CCB was able to secure river crossings over the Meuse at Namur and crossed on 5-6 September. From Namur they moved towards Liège down the Meuse Valley, overrunning retreating Germans as they fled. However, quick as the advance across Northern France and Belgium was, the German defense quickly stiffened as the German border grew closer. By 9 September, the Germans began to build roadblocks and stiffen their defense. The Siegfried Line was approaching and the Germans were going to defend their Fatherland. German battle groups were being formed from the retreating units and new battle groups like the Panzer Brigade 105 were being sent to the area to stem the tide. By 11-12 September, the German border was within sight and it was clear to the 3rd Armored Division that the move into Germany was going to be very different to their recent rapid advance. The division had learned a lot since coming ashore on 23 June and they would need every bit of that experience as they were now poised to attack the German soldiers' homeland. The Westwall was the next target, and with it would come the rain and mud of a German autumn season.

General Eisenhower and Field Marshal Montgomery visited the 3rd Armored Division at Warminster, England on February 25 1944. The officer on the extreme right is SHAEF Deputy Commander Arthur Tedder and next to him is the divisional commander, Major General Leroy Watson. Eisenhower is blocking Montgomery, who is peering into the turret. This M4 medium tank is named 'Hop Along', making it from Company H of either the 32nd or 33rd Armored Regiment.

Same setting as the above photograph, but now the officers are observing action on a firing range. Unclear if this is the same tank as above, but it is a Company H tank as evidenced by the 'H-6' marking on the lower right of the M4 medium tank.

CCA of the 3rd Armored in action on July 3 1944 near Saint-Clair-sur-l'Elle, France. A nervous GI looks up to the air as M4 medium tanks from three different 3rd Armored units form up. The tank closest to the cameraman is an HQ tank from 3rd Battalion, 32nd Armored Regiment as evidenced by the tank beginning with a '3' on the turret. The middle one has an 'O', making it a field observer tank of the 67th Armored Field Artillery Battalion, and the furthest tank is an I company tank from the 3rd Battalion, 32nd Armored Regiment.

A mix of 3rd Armored Division vehicles prepare for the further move inland in Normandy in late June, 1944. This is a mix of halftracks, trucks and even a motorcycle zooming by. Once the vehicles landed on shore from the LSTs they were prepared for action on land.

July 7, 1944, A M10 3in gun motor carriage
rumbles down a street in St. Fromond, France.
The tank destroyer, number B-21, belongs to
the 703rd Tank Destroyer Battalion, the organic
TD unit for the 3rd Armored.

The 3rd Armored was working with the 30th Infantry Division in the St. Fromond area. This picture was taken on July 10 1944 and shows an M5A1 light tank, 'B-12' moving past infantry and signal wiremen. Other images of this tank exist which allow us to identify it as a tank from the 2nd Battalion, 33rd Armored Regiment, CCB.

A well-known image taken on the outskirts of St. Fromond that shows two captured German Pz.Kpfw IV tanks of the 6th Company of SS Panzer Regiment 2 of the 2nd SS Panzer Division. The M4A1 medium tank approaching is named 'Derby' from Company D, 2nd Battalion, 33rd Armored Regiment, CCB.

An M5A1 light tank of Company C, 33rd Armored Regiment guards a corner in St. Fromond on July 11. This angle gives a good view of the contraption that was typical of 33rd Armored Regiment tanks. The prevailing opinion among experts is that it was to help deflect bullets from the bow gunner's MG position into trenches, but no proof of that has been found to date.

The scenes continue in St. Fromond as a mixed column of light tanks, jeeps, half-tracks and armored cars make their way through town onto various points of the front line. The M5A1 light tank is named 'Carol' and is fitted with the typical stowage equipment and materials carried by tankers.

Series of three photos showing three different vehicles from CCA moving out to support the division near Saint-Jean-de-Daye on July 11. The first photo shows an M2A1 half-track named 'Hellzapoppin' from Company H, 36th Armored Infantry Regiment leaving the camouflaged area that engineers have made on the side of the road. Note the sign on the lower left that says 'Oriole Blue', the code name for the 3rd Battalion, 32nd Armored Regiment.

The next vehicle out to meet the onrush of the Panzer Lehr Division counter-attack is an M4 medium tank with a composite hull of the 3rd Battalion, 32nd Armored Regiment. After just a few days of fighting the turret markings have already begun to fade.

The last vehicle photographed out of the camouflage area is an M10 3in gun motor carriage from the 703rd Tank Destroyer Battalion. Based on after-action reports of the unit, they claimed knocking out ten Panthers and one Pz.Kpfw. IV. This particular vehicle is numbered A21 and is named 'Accident', obviously making it from Company A.

To counter the hedgerows, the 3rd Armored Division employed their bulldozer tanks to assist in knocking down the earthen berms so the infantry and other vehicles could pass through. Here an M4 medium dozer tank named 'Here's Dot's Mom' from the 23rd Armored Engineer Battalion prepares to knock down a hedgerow.

Based on cine film that the signal photo company unit attached to the 3rd Armored Division took of this bulldozer tank and the photo number sequence, this could very well be same tank as above as it comes out from the other side of the hedgerow.

Near Le Desert on July 14, an M31 tank recovery vehicle prepares to tow away an M4 medium tank, Company G of the 32nd Armored Regiment to a maintenance facility. Note there is another M31 in front of the one hooked up to the M4. A motorcycle is also hitching a ride on the damaged M4.

Two of the numerous Panthers that the Panzer Lehr Division lost near Le Desert in their counter-attack. This photo shows the narrowness of the typical Normandy country roads which made tank warfare dangerous.

A well-known Panther named 'Ursula' of the Panzer Lehr Division knocked out in the 3rd Armored Division sector around Le Desert on July 11 by the 899th Tank Destroyer Battalion.

GIs get a closer look at the knocked-out 'Ursula' which shows a burned German tank crewman on the rear of the engine deck. This is a Panther A model.

Just a few yards behind 'Ursula' was 'Elna', another Panther A of the Panzer Lehr Division. Naming their tanks after their favorite girl was common practice at this time for a few Panzer Lehr tank commanders. Note the cracked armor under the GI standing by the main gun, a sign of a massive penetration shot.

The rear of 'Elna' is inspected by a curious GI. The powerful and feared Panther tank was a curiosity to American soldiers, especially when first encountered in the early Normandy battles.

A heavy truck and a flatbed trailer have been called in to tow away 'Ursula' for further inspection at a collection point to which it would be taken. Eventually the tanks would be scrapped for their metal.

Just outside Le Desert, the commander of the photo unit attached to the 3rd Armored, Lieutenant Thomas Noble, took a series of photos he labeled 'Removing Dead Germans from tanks'. This particular Panther is numbered 215, is named 'Ingrid' and is also from the Panzer Lehr Division. A combination of SS and Luftwaffe prisoners are assisting in removing the dead soldiers from the tank.

Just yards behind the previous Panther, 'Ingrid' was another Panther from the same unit but with no name or number discernible. The tank has been applied with an anti-magnetic material known as 'Zimmerit' to prevent the attachment of magnetic mines. Behind the Panther, the rear of a Funkpanzerwagen (Sd.Kfz.251.3) with its antenna can be seen.

The Sd.Kfz 251.3 noted above can now be seen with a famous Disney character applied on the side. An M1A1 wrecker from the 464th Ordnance Recovery Company has chains attached to pull it from the roadside.

The Sd.Kfz 251.3 has been moved off the road to make room for traffic and presumably for ordnance intelligence units to get a better look at it. The village itself looks like it has seen a recent battle. The symbol on the side of the engine compartment with the Scholze devil insignia has been attributed to vehicles of Panzer Grenadier Regiment 901.

Lieutenant Noble moved to the opposite side of the half-track for more photos and captured the Mickey Mouse logo once again. The items in the stowage bin near the front are extra track pads for the half-track.

Another Panther of the Panzer Lehr Division knocked out and left on the side of the road. The size of the crater in front of it may be indicative of an air bombardment that knocked this tank out in mid-July 1944, 3rd Armored Division sector.

An unidentified Panzerkampfwagen IV knocked out around St. Lo as per the writing on this photo from the 3rd Armored Division archives. The tank has suffered a catastrophic loss to the lower right hull. Again, note the narrow country roads and woods of the hedgerow country.

Continuing with Panthers of the Panzer Lehr lost around the Le Desert area is this Panther A, numbered 414. Burn marks near the gun mantlet show that this tank was in fact hit and suffered some sort of fire.

Soldiers from the 83rd Armored Reconnaissance have stopped to check out the charred remains of the above Panther. The large numbers used by Panzer Lehr for their Panthers are very apparent in this angle of the photo. (© *George H. Bloth Collection*)

Earlier a photo of Panther 215 'Ingrid' showed its dead soldiers being removed. Since then it has been moved to a collection point in a field somewhere in Normandy. These soldiers are also from the 83rd Armored Reconnaissance Battalion. (© *George H. Bloth Collection*)

Two of three soldiers from above have climbed aboard Panther 414 for a closer look and better photo opportunity. The Zimmerit applied to the front glacis is visible quite clearly in this frontal photo. (© *George H. Bloth Collection*)

An M4A1 medium tank of the 33rd Armored Regiment (note the bracket by the bow gunner's position) lays knocked out on a Normandy road, July/August 1944. Sandbags had been applied for extra frontal protection, but the low armor piercing shown was able to miss the sandbags and cause damage. A tow cable is attached for eventual removal.

Another M4A1 medium tank of the 33rd Armored Regiment knocked out along the road. The driver's position has taken a well-aimed shot via an armor-piercing shell. Again, the sandbags have provided no help to the crew in this case.

This is the same M4A1 as in the previous photo, showing the narrow country roads and concealment available for the enemy to ambush tanks as they traveled down the Normandy countryside. A 'D' can be made out on the turret, making this a 2nd Battalion, 33rd Armored Regiment vehicle.

Another similar view of a Normandy country road with two knocked-out M4 medium tanks of the 3rd Armored along the roadside. Typically the tanks, once knocked out, would be pushed aside for later retrieval so the attacking columns could continue their advance.

Yet another 3rd Armored Division tank knocked out along a Normandy country road. The markings are faint, but it could be a vehicle from Company G from either the 32nd or 33rd Armored Regiment. The driver's side has taken a hit right at head level, so hopefully he bailed out before that hit was received.

Key to the success of the armored and artillery units of the 3rd Armored Division was the use of L-4 'Grasshopper' planes for observation. Here pilot First Lieutenant Allen Knisley and observer First Lieutenant Robert Schultz of the 67th Armored Field Artillery Battalion prepare to take off for observation near Saint-Jean-de-Daye on July 20 1944.

While at rest near Saint-Jean-de-Daye in preparation for the next big push which would be Operation COBRA, Sergeant Joe DeMarco of the 165th Signal Photographic Company took several photos of the men of the various units of the 3rd Armored Division. The next several photos of soldiers at rest are taken at Saint-Jean-de-Daye around July 22 1944. Here is dispatch rider Private Robert Lane on a WLA motorcycle named 'Bombshell'.

Corporal John Burleson, driver of a tank in Company E, 32nd Armored Regiment, poses for a photograph in his M4A1 (76) medium tank. Burleson was a crew member of Clarence Smoyer in Normandy. Smoyer is famous for knocking out the Panther in Cologne at the cathedral.

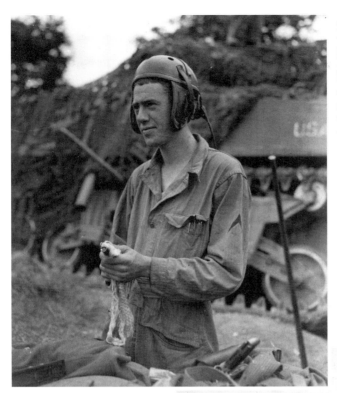

Another member of Company E 32nd Armored Regiment photographed was Corporal Hubert Foster. Foster is seen here in front of his tank while cleaning his personal weapons and gear. He is wearing the tanker coveralls and standard tanker helmet.

Sergeant Arthur Stolan, also from E/32nd, is pictured in the commander's hatch of his M4 tank while holding the handset known as the pork chop, likely for its shape. Sadly, Stolan and one of his crew members were killed just ten days later near Juvigny-le-Tertre as the next offensive started. He died of his wounds when his tank was hit.

Sergeant Dennis Donovan, a star football player at the University of Oregon before the war, became a tank commander in E/32nd. He can be seen here cleaning his pistol while posing for the photographer. Donovan was wounded several times and lost a few tanks, but he survived the war.

At this time Corporal Ralph Wedgewood was a crew member for Sergeant Donovan, but as the war progressed and casualties mounted, he himself would be promoted and also become a tank commander. Wedgewood is also cleaning his weapon or perhaps posing in front of the area where Donovan was photographed.

Sometimes the cameramen forgot to add captions or they didn't make it to the photo lab. Here is a case of one of those. The tanker is most likely an officer given the shoulder holster for his sidearm. He is wearing his helmet over his tanker helmet which is unplugged from the main radio.

An unnamed dispatch rider of the 3rd Armored Division aboard a 'Liberator' (Harley-Davidson WLA) motorcycle. This was named 'Raid', maybe from the 83rd Reconnaissance Battalion. Note the Spearhead patch on his leather helmet under the goggles.

Right: An unknown tank commander of E/32nd taken along with the other photos of the named soldiers on the previous pages. The men of Spearhead had been in action for less than a month, but the strain can be seen on their faces already.

Below: July 26 1944: aerial view of a 3rd Armored Division maintenance facility near Saint-Jean-de-Daye. At this location, 3rd Armored tanks were being fitted with T2 Douglas devices for crushing through the hedgerows.

A T2 Douglas device is prepared to be welded to an M4A1 (76). These devices were critical in smashing through the hedgerows and would prove vital for the upcoming Operation COBRA.

Major General Watson, at this time still in command of the division, talks with a junior officer about the installation of the T2 devices which were unique to the 3rd Armored Division.

A wide-angle view of the ordnance workshop in the town square as devices are welded to the tanks and the crews patiently wait for their tanks to be completed.

An M4 (75) and M4A1 (76) get fitted with devices as their crews wait. The tank closest to the camera is named 'Iron Mike' from I/32nd and is probably named after the tank commander.

The crew of this M4A1 (76) seem content to sit back and watch the ordnance men do their work and get the T2 device ready to weld onto the front of their tank. The tank to their right has already been completed with its installation.

Observing the installation of the T2 devices is the soon-to-be commanding general of the 3rd Armored Division, Maurice Rose, standing to the left of another 3rd Armored officer.

Satisfied that he has seen enough of the maintenance work, Major General Watson and his driver don their helmets and prepare to depart in the CG's jeep, armed with a .30 caliber machine gun on the passenger side. The M4 (75) tank 'Iron Mike' is directly behind them.

A rear view of the maintenance facility where the tanks seen in the previous images were being outfitted with the T2 Douglas devices for hedgerow-busting. The 3rd Armored Division was now ready for Operation COBRA.

July 26 1944: a German prisoner is brought in from the front around Marigny, France in a jeep with Colonel Truman Boudinot. Boudinot would soon be promoted to general and lead CCB of the 3rd Armored throughout the war.

An M8 75mm howitzer motor carriage of the 33rd Armored Reconnaissance Company takes the lead in moving through Montreuil, France as a bulldozer repairs shell-holes and clears debris, July 26 1944.

Most signal corps photos were staged and taken away from the front lines or when the action was quiet. Here five crew members of an M10 3in gun motor carriage (TD) smile for the camera under the comfort of their TD-covered foxhole. The tank destroyer has been fitted with sandbags on the front for extra protection and is from the 703rd Tank Destroyer Battalion.

A Ford GPA jeep from the 32nd Armored Reconnaissance Company moves past a severely damaged church in La Chapelle-en-Juger on July 27 1944. The back of the GPA has an identification panel draped to prevent Allied bombers from mistaking it for a German vehicle.

Captain Richard Campfield, at this time, July 31 1944, was still the company commander of E/32nd before being promoted to the 2nd Battalion of the 32nd Armored Regiment staff. Here he is giving a briefing during Operation COBRA to his company tank commanders before moving out.

This photo was taken right after the above photo so the cameraman must have been around a pre-deployment area where soldiers were resting before the big push. Here men sit around an M4 medium tank used as a field observation tank for the 67th Armored Field Artillery Battalion.

A common sight
in late July/
early August
in Normandy:
a knocked-out
and overturned
German Panther
tank. The tracks
that used to
adorn this can
be seen to the
left of the soldier
examining the
ruins. This tank
was knocked
out in the 3rd
Armored sector.

A pair of M5A1 light tanks of Company B, 33rd Armored Regiment race down a French road during the big attack around Marigny during COBRA. The first tank is numbered B-21 and an identification panel can be seen draped on the back.

This M5A1 light tank is interesting in a couple of ways. First it has markings of 3-11 on the back, features the bracket typical of the 33rd Armored Regiment and also an 'X' and 'HQ' unit markings on the front, most likely making this an HQ command tank of the 3rd Battalion, 33rd Armored Regiment. The man to the left of the tank commander also bears a marked resemblance to Colonel Dorrance Roysden from the 33rd Armored Regiment.

An M3A1 half-track towing a 37mm anti-tank gun passes a destroyed Sd.Kfz 7 mounted with a quad 20mm AA gun and a Marder tank destroyer through the ruins of Roncey, France. Based on the markings of the US half-track, the unit belongs to a maintenance company of the division.

An M4A1 (76) numbered D2 of the 32nd Armored Regiment and fitted with the T2 Douglas device and sandbags for frontal protection moves through a French town loaded with GIs on the rear. This was one of the first sixty M4A1 (76) models delivered to the division in time for Operation COBRA.

Somewhere in France in the 3rd Armored Division sector, one of numerous knocked-out German half-tracks litters the roadside. This particular vehicle appears to have been turned over in a small gully or shell-hole.

Marvin Mischnick who served as a cameraman with the 3rd Armored Division took this photo of a Jagdpanzer IV on a roadside with another not too far behind in the rear. The vehicle has been hit by two AP rounds that penetrated the bow armor.

An M4 medium tank of Company I, 1st Battalion, 33rd Armored Regiment leads a column of tanks and an M8 armored car down a French road during Operation COBRA. This particular tank was made by Baldwin Locomotive.

During late July and early August, the 3rd Armored Division was going head-to-head with the 2nd SS Panzer Division 'Das Reich' and also elements of the 1st SS Panzer Division. Here on the roadside, a soldier with the 3rd Armored took a photo of captured German Panther A numbered 333 from the SS Panzer Regiment 2 of the 2nd SS Panzer Division.

Maintenance men of the 3rd Armored begin to take apart a knocked-out German Panther in a field somewhere in Normandy.

These two photos show two different tanks of Company E, 32nd Armored Regiment knocked out in Juvigny-le-Tertre on August 1 or 2. Earlier in this chapter, Sergeant Arthur Stolan was featured. His tank was either this one or the bottom one; no confirmation has been made to date.

The M4 medium tank is still smoking from the hits it took. To the right is a German self-propelled gun that was involved in the action. The burn damage around the turret of the M4 tank reflects a massive fire that engulfed the vehicle. The rear shows the welding marks remnants of the fording stack.

On August 7, tanks from the 1st Battalion, 33rd Armored Regiment, companies F and I move out from Reffuveille to attack German units at Le Mesnil-Adelée. These units of the 3rd Armored Division also had armored infantry from the 3rd Battalion, 36th Armored Infantry Regiment and were known as Task Force King after the commander, Colonel Roswell King.

Taken just after the previous photo, this M4 medium tank is from the HQ section of Company I, 33rd Armored Regiment. Based on records of knocked-out 3rd Armored tanks, we know that this was one was lost just days later after an enemy hit caused a fire and explosion. In fact, post-war records that detailed searching for MIA remains reference this tank's serial number as being searched for remains among others days after it was lost.

Another photo from the previous sequence, an M4A1 (76) with T2 Douglas device awaits the call near Reffuveille to move out on the advance to meet the enemy. It appears that the cameraman got into a shell-hole for dramatic effect.

Private Edwin Larsen is photographed here on August 6 and was a member of a reconnaissance unit of the 32nd Armored Regiment. With a smoke in one hand and a loaded Thompson sub-machine gun in the other, he looks ready for anything the Germans may throw at him.

August 8: A T2 armored recovery vehicle pulls an M4 medium tank out of a ditch on the side of a French road. The crew from the disabled tank appears to be still around the tank, so it may have been a case of bad driving rather than being knocked out or hit by enemy fire.

Four American M4 tanks including a bulldozer tank sit ready in the background of the M4 medium tank in the foreground as they prepare to move out to meet the Germans around Couptrain, France on August 13 1944.

Also near Couptrain, a vehicular column of the 3rd Armored including an M8 75mm HMC and an M8 armored car watch a P-47 Thunderbolt strafe enemy targets before resuming their advance.

The photo censor markings prohibit us from identifying to which tank regiment from the 3rd Armored this M4A1 (76) with an early T20 turret and M1A1 gun belongs. However, based on the date of August 13 and location near Couptrain on the way to Ranes-Fromental, it is probably from TF Richardson of the 32nd Armored Regiment.

This photo was taken in Champéon and shows an M4 bulldozer tank casually moving through the streets taking time to greet civilians and it appears perhaps indulge in some French wine.

An American and French flag fly from the town square statue as newly-liberated French civilians greet an M5A1 light tank of an HQ unit of the 3rd Armored Division in Javron, France on August 13 1944.

Another view of the same town square of Javron above as an M8 75mm HMC from a recon unit makes its way through the town. This vehicle has been heavily fitted with sandbags on the front for extra protection from armor-piercing weapons.

According to the caption, this armored car knocked out two Mark IV tanks with their 37mm gun. It is a great side profile shot of an M8 armored car and its crew during a brief period of rest. This armored car belonged to the 32nd Armored Reconnaissance Company of the 3rd Armored Division.

A German Sd.Kfz .251 half-track lies smoldering among other vehicles in a column roadside near Carrouges, France on August 13 1944 where the 3rd Armored Division was fighting elements of the 1st SS Panzer Division. At this point the American armored advance in concert with tactical air strikes was wreaking havoc on German armored units.

An M5A1 light tank of the 32nd Armored Regiment leads a column through Carrouges, France on August 16. The light tank has spare tracks on the front. The tanker next to the commander in the hatch has his SMG pointed at the French civilians, but they do not appear too much of a threat.

According to the caption this French woman was a Nazi sympathizer and is being marched back to Pré-en-Pail, France past an M4 medium tank of the 3rd Armored Division. Part of the tank's name is seen as 'Robin...' but it sports the bracket typical of the 33rd Armored Regiment so it may belong to the reconnaissance company of the 33rd Armored. A bustle rack has been added to the rear of the turret.

An M4 medium tank of the 3rd Armored Division with a T2 Douglas device and frontal sandbag protection moves past a German 88mm anti-aircraft gun. Spare shells for perhaps the 88mm lay on the other side of the road.

The action around Fromental on August 16-17 for the 32nd Armored Regiment was intense and resulted in numerous tank losses for the regiment. Here, a tank from Company E, 32nd Armored Regiment moves past a knocked-out M4 medium tank on the outskirts of the village.

This photo was taken from almost the same spot as the previous one, on the outskirts of Fromental. Infantrymen of the 36th Armored Infantry pause while armor advances into the town. Note the two soldiers who have been killed in action in the ditch in the foreground.

This photo and the one below are the same Panther from the 1st SS Panzer Division knocked out in the vicious fighting around the Ranes-Fromental area during August 16-18. Numerous rounds have either penetrated or ricocheted off the glacis and side armor.

According to the history of the 703rd Tank Destroyer Battalion, this Panther was knocked out by tank destroyer crewman Corporal Joseph Juno at a range of 25 yards. Juno himself was killed when he exited the vehicle to help the wounded German tankers.

A Panzerkampfwagen IV of the 2nd SS Panzer Division sits abandoned after being knocked out in the Ranes-Fromental area. Foliage still hangs on the side of the tank and it has also been applied with a Zimmerit coating as well.

The fields of France in the 3rd Armored sector during August were rife with knocked out and abandoned German tanks. Here is another Panther Ausf.A that, based on the spare tracks on the turret, identifies this tank as belonging to the 1st SS Panzer Division. Fire from several hits has burned off the Zimmerit from the tank and also the rubber from the road wheels.

Another abandoned Panther Ausf.A, this time a Pz.Bef.Wg command tank in a well-concealed position in a hedgerow setting. The spare track hooks on the side most likely also make this a tank from the 1st SS Panzer Division.

This particular Panther Ausf.A has taken a massive hit on the turret causing a large hole and eventual fire that burned off a good portion of the Zimmerit. Note the tube on the side of the tank that contained the cleaning rods for the main gun.

Yet another German Panther Ausf.A left on the battlefield. Between the dominant Allied air power and fast-advancing armor of Operation COBRA, the German armor was being destroyed on the French countryside.

A German Sturmgeschütz III Ausf.G knocked out in a French town sometime in August 1944. The soldier photographed was with the divisional staff of the 3rd Armored so this photo was taken after the front lines had passed through. The markings indicate that the 974th Ordnance Evacuation Company has checked and cleared the vehicle.

British, Polish or even Canadian soldiers on a 3rd Armored Division tank? This M4 medium tank with extra armor on the turret appears to have the markings of E/32nd and has lost its tracks on one side. There are weld marks on the rear from a deep water-fording tank, making this one of the first tanks to come ashore at Normandy for the division. It also has markings that an ordnance recovery company has checked it out and is ready for removal.

An M4A1 (76) medium tank from the 32nd Armored Regiment, perhaps Company I based on the frontal markings, sits knocked out in a field. A woman and young children pose with the vehicle that helped liberate them in the summer of 1944. Based on the registration number, it is from the initial production batch from Pressed Steel Car.

An M4A1 medium tank from the 3rd Armored Division crosses the Seine River over a treadway pontoon bridge on August 26. The motor boat to the left of the bridge has the markings of the 23rd Armored Engineer Battalion and the photo censor has scribbled out the hedgerow-cutting device on the front.

A different angle of the same bridge crossing over the Seine as above. This time the censor has scribbled the riverbank from where the unit is crossing so as not to give away the location. A column of M3A1 half-tracks makes their way across under the watchful eye of the engineers.

With the Falaise Pocket closed on 18 August, the race across France to Belgium had commenced. The hedgerows gave way to open fields and 'tank country'. Here an M4A1 (76) fires at a retreating German convoy during the drive towards Sedan on 31 August.

The 3rd Armored advance to Belgium was swift across Northern France. Here a tank (I-33) from CCB, 33rd Armored Regiment advances past burning German vehicles near Malplaquet, France on 2 September. This particular tank would be knocked out by German artillery just a few months later at Hastenrath, Germany.

A German Tiger 1 tank being inspected by curious French civilians and American soldiers in Marle, France on 2 September. The Tiger 1 has been spray-painted for camouflage.

Ghlin, Belgium is a village on the outskirts of Mons and on 3 September elements of TF Mills of the 33rd Armored Regiment were advancing quickly through it on the way to Mons. An M4A1 watches tanks advance towards their objective as smoke billows in the background; a sign of where the action is.

Another photo from the same action as in the previous picture. An M3A1 half-track is preparing to join the advance up the road as the smoke intensifies up ahead.

As 3rd Armored units began to reach the small towns around Mons, the Mons pocket had been sealed and thousands of retreating Germans would be taken prisoner. Here in the suburbs of Mons is an M4 medium tank with the T2 Douglas device attached making its way through jubilant Belgian crowds.

Along the same street corner as the previous photo is an M31 Armored Recovery Vehicle making its way through the crowd. The faces of the Belgian civilians show the elation of liberation after four years of German rule.

Here 3rd Armored headquarter jeeps move between M4 medium tanks, the one on the right being an M4A1 (76) on the outskirts of Mons. Note the abundance of armed French and Belgian resistance fighters probably assisting the tankers with directions and locations of German units.

Brigadier Doyle Hickey of CCA leans on his jeep and watches a column led by an M4 medium tank move through the city of Mons on 3 September.

On the French/Belgian border, a signal corps cameraman took this photo of an M4A1 (76) medium tank with both sandbags for frontal protection and a welded T2 Douglas device. The tank also has the D82081 turret. There is also a well-known photo of General Rose in this exact spot.

Just outside Mons on 2 September sits a burning M4 medium tank from Spearhead that is being passed by an M5A1 light tank. According to the signal corps caption, it was the first Spearhead tank lost in Belgium.

An M4 medium tank fires down the Rue de Fétinne towards the Englebert Tire Factory in Liège, Belgium on 8 September.

A great photo of a command meeting between (left to right) Colonel Frederic Brown (divisional artillery), Lieutenant Colonel George Garton (391st Armored Field Artillery Battalion) and Colonel Truman Boudinot, CCB commander on the outskirts of Liège on 8 September.

On the outskirts of Liège, in Chênée, a young Belgian woman throws flowers to the crew of an M4A1 (76) tank that has liberated them. A squad of 'blitzdoughs', as the 36th Armored Infantry soldiers were known, sits on the back and enjoys the fanfare. The tank shows the typical graffiti with which the liberated Belgians had adorned them using chalk.

An M7 105mm Howitzer Motor Carriage number 'C3' from the 67th Armored Field Artillery Battalion moves through Namur, Belgium in early September past cheering Belgian civilians. The crew commander in the middle appears to be consulting his map.

Another liberated Belgian town and the infamous chalk signatures on the vehicles. Here an M4 medium tank of the 32nd Armored Regiment stops to receive some local goodies from two Belgian gentlemen.

The caption on this photo indicated that it was taken in Liège and it shows another M4 medium tank of the 3rd Armored making its way through the city.

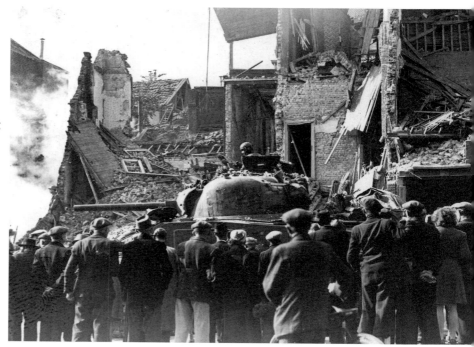

'F23', an M4 medium tank with TF Mills of the 33rd Armored Regiment makes its way off a treadway pontoon bridge after crossing the River Meuse near Namur.

Another photo taken at the same treadway pontoon bridge crossing of the Meuse as in the previous picture. In this photo we see another bridge is under construction by the engineers to help speed the advance over the river. The engineer is helping guide the tank driver keep his tracks inside the treadway. A line of vehicles wait their turn on the far side.

An M3A1 medical half-track from the 33rd Armored Regiment makes its way over the same treadway pontoon bridge as above. In the distance a bulldozer tank prepares to cross as well.

The 486th Anti-Aircraft Battalion of the 3rd Armored Division along with units of the 67th Armored Field Artillery Battalion encountered two different trains at Braine, France near the end of August. One train had four Tiger 1 tanks (pictured here) and the other had supply cars and a Panzer IV tank. Both trains were knocked out and captured.

FFI men inspect one of the Tiger 1s on one of the trains at Braine. The Tigers were being shipped back to Germany for repairs and reassignment to other units.

Here is a photo of the other train that contained the supplies and the lone Panzer IV tank, which has been heavily camouflaged from aerial bombardment. The supplies contained items such as perfume, liquor and women's stockings.

A wide-angle view of the train that had the four Tigers, all clearly visible here. The front Tiger turned its turret to counter the attack from the Spearhead units, but to no avail.

Near Liège, crossing the River Meuse is the tank of the acclaimed tank ace of the 3rd Armored Division, Sergeant Lafayette Pool of Company I, 32nd Armored Regiment. The M4A1 (76) is being guided by an engineer as it makes its way across the treadway pontoon bridge. In about ten days, Pool's tank would be hit, he would lose a leg and his war was over as he was sent home.

American jeeps and half-tracks of the 3rd Armored speed through Namur as civilians wave them on among flying Belgian flags.

A 3rd Armored tank with not a T2 Douglas device, but rather a Cullen hedgerow-cutter makes its way through a Belgian town during early September. The jubilant crowds of the liberated Belgian towns would soon be replaced with the unfriendly welcome of the German Siegfried Line.

CHAPTER TWO

As the armored columns of the Spearhead raced across Belgium and liberated the jubilant cities, they were now suddenly faced with the Siegfried Line or Westwall of Germany. Probing actions at various points of the line began on 12 September. By 1452 hours on the same day, Task Force Lovelady of CCB crossed the German border at the town of Roetgen. It was the first German town to fall to an enemy invader since Napoleon.

Meanwhile, Task Force X, commanded by Colonel Leander Doan of CCA, was assembling in the woods near Eynatten, south of Aachen, with the target of Oberforstbach. Here the Westwall defenses were about 1,000 yards behind the actual border. The plan was for the attached infantry to secure the high ground by the Westwall defenses and hold, while the engineers would breach the defenses and the tanks could then advance through without impediment. The Westwall featured numerous concrete pillboxes and bunkers, dragons' teeth tank barriers and this particular area of the line at Oberforstbach gave the Germans the high ground with an unobstructed view of the attackers. The attack started on 13 September and very quickly one of the flail mine tanks that Task Force X had sent through became stuck and had to be pulled out by two very brave medium tank crews. Tanks were being knocked out by precise German anti-tank fire and the infantry slogged their way through the Westwall defenses. In addition to the GIs of the 36th Armored Infantry Regiment, the 1st Battalion, 26th Infantry Regiment of the famed 1st Infantry Division was also attacking with Task Force X. The infantry attack progressed towards Nutheim, while the tankers, after losing several tanks to mines and anti-tank fire, were able to reach Nutheim as well. By the morning of the 14th, CCA continued the attack and a second line of defenses were reached. Task Force Y of CCA joined the attack and by 15 September, CCA had reached Munsterbuch. It was during these battles that the famed tank ace of the 32nd Armored Regiment, Sergeant Lafayette Pool, had his tank knocked out, was seriously wounded and left the war with an amputated leg.

During this same time, CCB was piercing their area of the Westwall as well. They were on the right flank of the advance and were dealing with the area from Roetgen to Rott, while Task Force 2 (Lovelady) of CCB was tasked with taking Rott, and Task Force 1 (King) was given Kornelimünster. German bunkers and tank barriers were encountered near Schmidthof and by 1500 on 15 September, Task Force 2 was just beyond Büsbach. Task Force 1 was held up near Giesch Creek by German anti-tank fire coming from the Mausbach area, the area of the second line of Siegfried Line defenses. Mopping-up in this general area continued until 23 September and the division was firmly entrenched in about half of the German city of Stolberg. The division was also spread out in the neighboring areas of Mausbach and Breinig. The division was physically exhausted and the vehicles were in dire need of replacement and general maintenance.

Initially Stolberg was split in half between the Americans and Germans. Constant mortar and shellfire was the daily and nightly occurrence in the area until Stolberg was fully controlled by the 3rd Armored Division. CCA had settled in the area of Breinig, while CCB was between there and Kornelimünster. The remaining divisional troops were located in Büsbach and Mausbach, with headquarters at the Prym Mansion. The road from Büsbach to Stolberg was a literal alley of German 88mm fire. Morning reports for the divisional units during the late September and October time frames are rife with the daily mention of men being wounded by shellfire, usually during the evening hours. The German artillery fire from Düren was constant and an unfriendly reminder that the Americans were now on German soil. However, for the most part as October began and continued on, it was a period of relative quiet for the division in this area. Replacements continued to arrive at the front lines and vehicles, mostly the tanks, were repaired and made ready for the next battle. Engineers cleared the bunkers that had been taken in the September battles and destroyed the remaining dragons' teeth with explosives and bulldozer tanks. The one instance of major action was around 19 October when Task Force Hogan of the 33rd Armored Regiment was tasked to assist the 1st Infantry Division with the capture of Aachen, specifically around Lousberg Hill. The weather at this time was cold, damp and rainy and the German houses around Stolberg were welcome sanctuaries for the men of Spearhead. Yet they knew this brief respite would not last. By November the VII Corps was ready for an offensive to push the lines out further into the Reich. The newly-arrived 104th Infantry Division bolstered the lines around the 3rd Armored and plans began for the next move.

Beyond the 3rd Armored lines was the natural defense barrier of the River Roer. Blocking the Roer were the well-entrenched German defenses centered on the Hamich-Hastenrath ridges that barred access to the Roer and Cologne plains. The Germans had built up these areas with minefields, bunkers and anti-tank strongpoints. Each village and town had in essence become a defensive strongpoint. The G-2 of VII Corps had noticed that the Germans were switching out the 12th Volksgrenadier Division with the 47th Infantry and saw an opportunity for an attack. The objective would be the ridges north-east of the road connecting Hamich to Hastenrath and the offensive was slated for 16 November. Recent wet weather would prove a challenge to the tracked vehicles of the 3rd Armored. The attack would be led by the 1st and 2nd battalions of the 33rd Armored Regiment, CCB, Task Force Mills and Lovelady respectively.

By 16 November at 1115 hours a break in the weather allowed for Allied bombers to fly their pre-attack bombardment mission over the area. In addition, artillery fire from the other Spearhead tank battalions and field artillery units provided support from the Stolberg area. At 1300, the attack then jumped off from the areas around Mausbach. Task Force Lovelady was assigned to take the towns of Werth and Kottenich, while Task Force Mills was assigned the towns of Scherpenseel and Hastenrath. On the right, Task Force Lovelady took their initial objective of Kottenich quite quickly and moved to Werth where the 104th Infantry Division would meet them. However, on the left flank, Task Force Mills ran into immediate trouble after running right into the middle of a minefield. In conjunction with the muddy terrain, tanks were disabled by mines or just plain stuck in the mud. The maintenance soldiers bravely removed vehicles under intense enemy fire. On just the first day of the attack, Task Force Mills lost sixteen medium tanks. By 17 November elements had finally reached Scherpenseel, and Hastenrath would not be entered until the 18th. Losses among the officers in the battalion for Task Force Mills were extremely heavy on the 18th; Lieutenant Colonel Herbert Mills, the task force commander, was killed by enemy artillery fire. He was replaced by the CCB commander, Colonel John Welborn. While Task Force Lovelady had things relatively under control at Werth, the towns of Scherpenseel and Hastenrath were the scenes of bitter fighting, intense bazooka fire from the Germans and constant counter-attacks. The advance and gains made by the 1st and 104th Infantry divisions on either side of the 3rd Armored had in essence pinched out the 3rd Armored by the end of 20 November. At the start of the offensive, the two tank battalions of CCB that were engaged started with 103 tanks and by the end of the four-day battle were down to 28 effective tanks. Losses were attributed to mines, anti-tank and artillery fire and also tanks stuck in the muddy terrain.

Shortly after this fierce battle by CCB, Task Force Richardson of CCA was tasked with a mission to secure the high ground between Frenz and Langerwehe. CCA was given the 2nd Battalion of the 47th Infantry, 9th Infantry Division to help with the attack that would start on 25 November. The attack was launched between two sets of railroad tracks and initially had success with Hücheln secured on the first night. Yet again, the muddy conditions would prove as great an obstacle as the German defenses. The next day, with mud on the left flank and anti-tank fire on the right, twelve of the thirteen attacking tanks were bogged down. The infantry was forced to take on the fight on their own and actually reached their objective without the 3rd Armored tanks. The landscape looked like one from the First World War: mud and craters with no room to move for the bogged-down tanks. In one field alone, the engineers removed more than 100 mines. The tanks of Task Force Richardson eventually rejoined the lines of CCA after this brief yet brutal attack around Hücheln.

Before the 3rd Armored Division was to be pulled out of the lines in December to stem the German counter-attack in the Ardennes, VII Corps had one more small mission for them. This time, CCR comprising Task Force Hogan from the 33rd Armored Regiment and Task Force Kane from the 32nd Armored Regiment would be tasked with loosening up the German lines around Echtz, Hoven, Geich and Obergeich. These towns needed to be cleared for the eventual advance to Düren and beyond. Once again, GIs from the 9th Infantry Division would be called on to help, this time from the 60th Infantry Regiment. Over the course of 10 to 12 December, CCR would be engaged in another round of battles that featured minefields, muddy terrain and stubborn German defenses of small German towns. Task Force Hogan made the initial advance through Obergeich where they encountered mines before reaching Geich. Task Force Kane battled towards Echtz against stubborn defenses before making their way to Hoven by 12 December with assistance from Task Force Hogan who had finally cleared Geich.

After another brief yet intense action with the enemy, CCR rejoined their fellow Spearheaders in the rear near Mausbach and began to make plans for a quiet Christmas. Men attended shows, enjoyed hot chow and caught up on mail as they prepared for a quiet holiday season. However, the German attack in the Ardennes, the Battle of the Bulge, would ruin their plans and thrust the Spearhead right smack in the middle of the action. By 18 December, the first units of the division were on the move to Belgium to serve as an initial stopgap measure for the American Army in their assigned sector and then once they had blunted the German attack they would go on the offensive to kick the Germans back into their homeland. The 3rd Armored was about to face some of the toughest German tank units and deal with cold and snowy weather that no one could have forecast. The Spearhead was on the move again; this time in the wrong direction.

Task Force Lovelady of CCB crossed the German border at Roetgen on 10 September 1944. The signal corps cameraman on the left is T/5 Leon Rosenman of the 165th Signal Photographic Company who was attached to the 3rd Armored. He is being interviewed by T.R. Henry of the *Washington Star*, a war correspondent covering the rapid advance. An M10 3in tank destroyer sits behind them, carefully looking down the road into Germany.

A wider view of the same location as above with an M4 medium tank of Company D, 33rd Armored Regiment now viewable. Crossing the German border was an obvious monumental event for the division and the American Army and that would explain the presence of the war correspondent.

An M4 medium tank from the 3rd Armored with an M31 (T2) Armored Recovery Vehicle close behind makes its way through the streets of Stolberg to move into a fighting position. There is movie footage of this event as well, and the soldier to the right of the frame who is cut off a bit appears to be the motion picture cameraman recording the event.

This photo is dated 30 September and, according to the caption, the bulldozer was moving dirt to cover the doors of the bunker so that it couldn't be re-used by the Germans. This area was firmly in American hands by this date, but the Germans were launching counter-attacks so the American units decided to play it safe and prevent their re-use.

An uncaptioned photo from the 3rd Armored after-action reports that shows a knocked-out M4 medium tank of Company H, 33rd Armored Regiment, Task Force Hogan somewhere in the area of Stolberg. The countryside pictured is typical of the area in which the 3rd Armored fought in the fall of 1944.

A German Panther tank photographed in front of a German house near Mausbach. The Panther belonged to the II./Panzer-Regiment 33 of the 9th Panzer Division. The Germans lost nine tanks on 17 September in their attempt to retake Mausbach.

Outside of the Stolberg area a mortar unit is engaged in steady action to support infantry and tank units at the front lines. Based on the number of shells around them, they have been quite busy.

This photo appears to have been taken after engineers have blown up a number of dragons' teeth to make a path for tanks of Task Force X of the 3rd Armored to pass through on 13 September. The rebar from the demolished blocks can be seen at the front of the path.

An M4 medium tank that has suffered a hit so damaging that the turret has been blown off. Based on the landscape and the bunker in the background, this is near the area of the Westwall where the 3rd Armored pierced the defenses but suffered heavy casualties in tanks and men. The front bracket unique to the 33rd Armored Regiment can be seen on this tank. (© *George H. Bloth Collection*)

An M4A1 (76) that has been hit and burned near a fence line in September 1944. Note how even the ground area around the tank has been damaged by the fire, burning fuel, etc. (© *George H. Bloth Collection*)

The same tank as shown in the previous photo but from the other side. The M4A1 (76) features the D82081 ventless turret style. What looks like a hole from an armor-piercing shell can be seen around where the loader would have been sitting. (© *George H. Bloth Collection*)

Another view taken at the Westwall evidenced by the dragons' teeth in the background. Here is an M8 armored car of a reconnaissance unit that has taken a catastrophic hit. The soldier who took these photos was with the 83rd Reconnaissance Battalion, so this vehicle probably belonged to his buddies. (© *George H. Bloth Collection*)

Around Stolberg a tank crew sits near their tank and a bunker they now call home. This particular spot is alongside a railroad track outside of Stolberg in September 1944.

Engineers of a unit in the 3rd Armored sector stand on a captured Panther of Panzer Brigade 105 at Büsbach. Although the caption dated the image 24 December 1944, this Panther was lost on 16 September 1944 after an engagement with American tanks of the 3rd US Armored Division. We know that two Panthers of Pz.Abt. 2105 were engaged at Büsbach on 16 September; one was the tank of the battalion's adjutant.

Soldiers inspect an M4 medium tank near the Westwall that has taken a devastating hit on the loader's side, smack in the middle of the hull. The gun is in full recoil and has remnants of a hedgerow-cutter previously attached. This shot was probably catastrophic to most of the crew, if not all of them. Markings make this tank from Company E of the 32nd Armored Regiment which lost several tanks in mid-September 1944, this being one of them. (© *George H. Bloth Collection*)

Crew members of an M8 armored car perform maintenance in a field in Germany, fall of 1944. Note the camouflaged vehicle in the background, probably making this a headquarters area. The markings on the rear of this M8 look to be of the 67th Armored Field Artillery Battalion. (© *George H. Bloth Collection*)

Two armor-piercing shells have left their mark between the assistant driver's and driver's position of this M4A1 (76) medium tank. This hit was probably catastrophic for the two men if they were still in the vehicle when hit. (© *George H. Bloth Collection*)

A damaged M4 medium tank undergoing repairs somewhere near Stolberg, fall of 1944. The track to the tank appears to be to the left of the vehicle. The maintenance units of the 3rd Armored were able to return damaged vehicles back to the front lines at amazing speed. (© *George H. Bloth Collection*)

The downtime in the Stolberg area after the breaching of the Siegfried Line and pushing the Germans back allowed the 3rd Armored to perform activities like the awarding of medals from earlier action. Here, on 4 October, Major General Maurice Rose awards medals to Spearhead men for their bravery in action in France.

Outside of Stolberg near Vicht on 4 October a headquarters unit of a tank unit sets up encampment near the safety of trees and a small valley. Among the tents are a half-track, a jeep and an M8 Howitzer Motor Carriage.

October 10, Corporal Cosimo Miranda of a 3rd Armored unit in Stolberg prepares grenades for distribution to other soldiers of his unit. Men behind him appear to be preparing gear and ammunition as well.

This photo was taken right after the above picture and it shows two soldiers, probably with the 36th Armored Infantry Regiment, getting their ammunition and personal gear ready for a patrol in the Stolberg sector. Both men are armed with Thompson sub-machine guns.

In the rear lines, the 3rd Armored sent their vehicles for repair by their divisional maintenance units or, if need be, the VII Corps of First Army assigned units that could deal with more advanced or intensive repairs. A whole assortment of vehicles can be seen in this picture: half-tracks, a wrecker, tanks and trucks.

M7 105mm self-propelled howitzers of the 391st Armored Field Artillery Battalion provide fire support on 14 October for the siege of Aachen, according to the caption. The 319st typically was assigned to CCB of the 3rd Armored during the war.

Taken in the same series as the photo above, but this time Sergeant DeMarco took a photo of a 155mm howitzer firing from a camouflaged position. The 991st Field Artillery Battalion was supporting the 3rd Armored Division at this time, 13 October.

Two photos of crews from the 486th Anti-Aircraft Battalion of the 3rd Armored Division. According to the caption, the men of this M15A1 half-track knocked out a Panzer IV tank and a supply truck in the advance across Belgium.

Another crew of an M15A1 half-track of the 486th AA Battalion. The M15A1 was equipped with one M1 automatic 37mm gun and two water-cooled .50 caliber M2 Browning heavy machine guns.

A well-known photograph of Company F, 36th Armored Infantry GIs aboard a sandbagged M4 of the 3rd Armored in Stolberg on 14 October. The GI second from the left was KIA just a month later around Mausbach on 17 November. However, on this date, this company of the 36th Armored Infantry was attached to Task Force Hogan, making this tank from the 3rd Battalion, 33rd Armored Regiment.

The exact tank and men from above, but now the cameraman has requested an 'action shot', yet obviously staged given the previous photo. It was common practice for the signal corps' cameramen to request certain types of shots from their photo subjects.

This photo is a testament to the number of shells the 3rd Armored was expending at this time around Stolberg.

The weather turned nasty in the fall of 1944 as the men in the Hürtgen Forest could attest, but in the area of Stolberg it was no different. Here a contraption made out of wooden boards has been attached to this jeep with chains to help smooth out some rough areas. Note the rifle-holder for the driver's weapon on the outside of the jeep.

In October, around the 24th, the 703rd Tank Destroyer Battalion switched out their old M10 3in gun motor carriages for the up-gunned M36 90mm gun motor carriage. The difference in size of the guns is clearly visible in this photo.

On the Auf da Mühle of Stolberg sits a knocked-out M4 medium tank of Company G, 33rd Armored Regiment. The tank still has the remnants of its deep wading trunk that was installed to help land on the Normandy beaches in June of 1944.

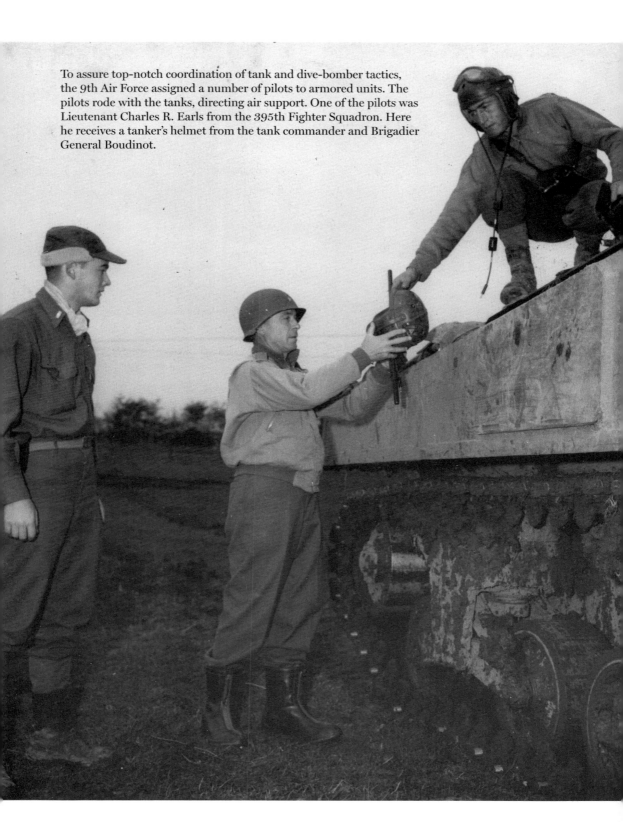

To assure top-notch coordination of tank and dive-bomber tactics, the 9th Air Force assigned a number of pilots to armored units. The pilots rode with the tanks, directing air support. One of the pilots was Lieutenant Charles R. Earls from the 395th Fighter Squadron. Here he receives a tanker's helmet from the tank commander and Brigadier General Boudinot.

Lieutenant Charles R. Earls enters a tank to assist as a liaison officer between his unit and the 3rd Armored Division. Behind the pilot is Brigadier General Truman E. Boudinot, commander of CCB. Earls would be killed in action on 19 November 1944.

An undated photo from the 3rd Armored Division archives with no location given, but given the buildings in the background, most likely somewhere in the Stolberg general area and lost in the fall of 1944.

These men were with a maintenance unit and were photographed in the Kornelimünster/Walheim area in October 1944. Here they are seen on top of an M4 medium tank and an M5A1 light tank.

This is the M4A1 (76) with D82081 turret that was to the right of the M5A1 in the previous photo. According to the caption on both photos, the men were performing maintenance on the communications equipment in each tank.

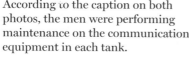

To counter the muddy conditions, tanks started to be fitted with extended end connectors, or 'duckbills'. Here a crew of a 3rd Armored Division tank gets fitted on 31 October in the rear of the front lines near Stolberg.

An M3A1 half-track of what is probably a headquarters unit, given that the tarp sits roadside in the streets of Stolberg.

An M31 armored recovery vehicle of the 32nd Armored Regiment tows an M3 half-track through the water and mud near Stolberg on 24 October.

Apparently this platoon of M5A1 light tanks doesn't scare this wandering cow outside of Stolberg. The tanks are from Company C, 32nd Armored Regiment and the first one in line. 'Comic' can be seen in signal corps movie footage in action around Villiers-Fossard on June 30 1944. This photo was taken on 2 November.

A knocked-out German Panther, probably from the 9th Panzer Division or Panzer Brigade 105 in the general area of Stolberg in the fall of 1944. The Panther has a coat of Zimmerit applied which has begun to fall off the turret. Note the tube for the gun cleaning rod that has been dented in.

Maintenance men of the 3rd Armored work on an M4A1 (76) in Walheim, Germany on 25 October. The transmission has been removed and hoisted by a wrecker in order for the work crew to do their maintenance. The D82081 turret configuration features a change where the loader's hatch was moved over to the commander's position and the commander's hatch was moved over to the loader's position. This was unique to the 33rd Armored Regiment tanks.

A trooper with the 3rd Armored cleans his Thompson SMG under the watchful eye of a German goat in the ruins of Mausbach on 29 October. As was typical of the American GI, he is using his helmet as a seat.

Same location as above photo and the German goat has attracted another GI, Corporal Sidonis Peis, who is offering some gum to the interested goat.

Two tanks of Company H, 32nd Armored Regiment, Task Force Richardson set up in roadblock positions outside of Stolberg on 29 October. It was typical for the tanks to park next to houses where the crews could sleep in warm quarters but still be close to their tanks.

Tank 'E-1' of the 33rd Armored Regiment lays knocked out around Stolberg on 30 October. According to the caption, it was hit by a German Panzer IV whose hits killed the American driver and set it on fire, but the M4 stayed in the fight and knocked out the German tank. The driver's compartment has taken two direct hits.

While the stalemate at Stolberg continued throughout October, men of the 23rd Armored Engineer Battalion continued to work on destroying the dragons' teeth defenses around the area. Here an M4 'dozer tank is simply pushing dirt over the obstacles to make a path for tanks and other vehicles to pass over.

Not to be outdone by their 'dozer tank counterpart, these engineers are placing explosives on a row of dragons' teeth to make a pathway through the defenses.

Behind an M12 155mm gun motor carriage of the 991st Field Artillery Battalion, serving with the 3rd Armored Division, the crew has displayed two 155mm shells. On the left is an American shell and on the right a captured German shell.

From the same gun on the previous page, but now the photographer has stepped back to catch the 155mm gun in action. The crew has named their vehicle 'Adolf's Assassin'. This action was photographed on 4 November outside Stolberg.

Dispatch rider with the 3rd Armored watches his bearings being adjusted by a maintenance man in Stolberg on 6 November. The motorcycle is a Harley-Davidson WLA 'Liberator'. Although the bike is covered in mud and dust, there are some great details to be seen. A .30 caliber ammunition case is being used to hold up the bike under the skid plate. The name 'NO RANK' has been painted as a nickname on the gas tank.

Outside the Stolberg area a building smokes from an artillery shell, while soldiers work on a tank at a roadblock position. This photo gives a good representation of the muddy conditions experienced by the 3rd Armored at this time.

In early November, a tank crew of an M4A3 (75) sits with a jeep and medical truck to listen to and record the results of the 1944 presidential election.

The results are in from the above election monitoring! Two soldiers make note on a sign outside of Stolberg on 7 November.

Great crew shot of a tank crew from 2nd Platoon, Company G, 32nd Armored Regiment outside Stolberg in the fall of 1944. Note the differences in clothing for the crew, and also the foliage applied to the tank for camouflage.

A photo of the entire 2nd Platoon, Company G, 32nd Armored Regiment commanded by Second Lieutenant Roger Jensen. They are photographed in front of an M4 medium tank in Stolberg.

Second Lieutenant Jensen of G/32nd photographed a lot around Stolberg in the fall of 1944. Here he took a photograph of a German Panther of the I./Pz.Rgt. 24, attached to Kampfgruppe Bayer of 116. Pz.Divison.

Same tank as above, but not as good quality a picture as that taken by Jensen. Two of the first digits of the tank can be seen, '22_', making it a 2nd Company tank.

Jensen had himself photographed with a German Panther of the 9th Panzer Division outside Stolberg near the Gressenich-Dieplinchen area. The tank was knocked out in mid-September, probably on the 16th or 17th.

Here Jensen is photographed with a German Jagdpanzer IV that in other photos the 1st Infantry Division claimed credit for the kill. The 1st Infantry was working closely with the 3rd Armored in this area so either unit could have claimed the kill.

Jensen took this shot of D-34 of the 32nd Armored Regiment moving down a road in Stolberg. He noted the photo was taken sometime between September and December of 1944 and the street is in front of the 1st Battalion, 32nd Armored command post.

Sergeant Hoover, platoon leader of 3rd Platoon, Company G, 32nd Armored in front of a German Panther by the Hotel Heeren in Welkenraedt which is in Belgium near the German border. Jensen's company would have been in this area and he took this photo of the tank which has been adorned with comical graffiti by the GIs in the area.

Three M-36 90mm GMCs prepare for a big push on 16 November in Büsbach, Germany. These vehicles are from Company A, 703rd Tank Destroyer Battalion.

Near Stolberg on 14 November, Private Leo Lapoint, a tanker with Company G, 33rd Armored Regiment takes a moment to catch up on letters from home on the rear of his tank. Note the other tanks down the road in the usual formation when occupying a city street.

The 3rd Armored units not participating in the assault on Hastenrath and Werth areas beginning on 16 November were used in a fire support capacity. Here, outside Breinig, Germany, tanks of the 32nd Armored Regiment fire in support of their comrades in the 33rd Armored Regiment.

In addition to tank fire support, field artillery units also participated in the bombardments of 16 November. Here in Mausbach a battery supplied with rockets prepares to fire in support of the 3rd Armored advance.

M4 (105) Sherman assault guns fire in support of the 3rd Armored from the cover of woods on the second day of the assault on Hastenrath, 17 November. The photo gives a good idea of the muddy conditions faced by the assault forces at this time.

Dwight Ellet of the 165th Signal Photographic Company took a series of photos of Company I, 32nd Armored Regiment firing in support of the assault on 17 November outside the area of Stolberg. Three additional tanks can be seen further down the firing line.

An M4 medium tank named 'Ink Spots', Company I, 32nd Armored Regiment fires in support of the assault behind a stack of empty shells which attests to the number of rounds that were fired. Company I and its sister company in the 3rd Battalion, 32nd Armored Regiment would lead an assault near the end of the month and would suffer a large number of knocked-out tanks due to mines and anti-tank fire after becoming stuck in mud.

Another view of 'Ink Spots' as crew members load shells to their fellow tanker. Note the tank has I-32 on the turret, but I-8 on the rear of the tank. Again, note the muddy conditions in which the tanks were forced to maneuver.

A haggard-looking soldier, Private Bernard Cohen, radio and scout man of a 3rd Armored recon unit awaits communication from the front lines for relay to headquarters outside of Mausbach on 17 November during the 3rd Armored assault on Hastenrath and Werth areas.

Pictured here is Colonel Frederick Brown, the divisional artillery commander for the 3rd Armored Division calling for an artillery strike from his jeep outside Mausbach, Germany. This photograph was taken during the assault in the Hastenrath and Werth areas.

Soldiers of the 3rd Armored and 104th Infantry Division consult maps outside of Werth on 18 November when action was intense in this area. The jeep is fitted with sandbags and also blankets to help with the cold and wind on the sides of the vehicle.

An engineer with the 3rd Armored Division sweeps for mines around a dead German soldier and knocked-out M5A1 light tank outside of Werth on 18 November.

Another engineer from the 3rd Armored with a minesweeper behind the M5A1 light tank in the picture above. Based on the fact that the tank has already lost its tracks and he is sweeping behind the tank, this photo is most likely staged.

Another view of the 3rd Battalion, 32nd Armored Regiment's firing support area outside Mausbach during the support of the 33rd Armored Regiment in their late November assault.

A closer view of the previous photo showing an M4 of the 32nd Armored Regiment preparing to fire in support of the assault at Hastenrath and Werth.

Probably the same tank as above, given that it was the next sequential photo that Sergeant DeMarco took. Tankers load shells into their M4 in preparation for the next barrage. Note the used shell containers being utilized as a walking path in the muddy field.

A better view of how useful the spent ammo cases were in dealing with the muddy conditions. The 3rd Armored tankers make a dry road to counter the mud, while a stack of fresh shells sits nearby, ready to be thrown over to the German lines.

A great shot of tank and infantry in action together outside Werth, Germany on 19 November. The soldiers and tank are with the 104th Infantry Division and 33rd Armored Regiment respectively.

An M3A1 armored half-track of the 3rd Armored rumbles through the town of Werth on 20 November. By this time Werth had been cleared, but action continued in the town of Hastenrath.

Just a few days after the battles at Werth and Hastenrath, the 3rd Battalion, 32nd Armored Regiment with support from the 47th Infantry Regiment of the 9th Infantry Division attacked toward Hücheln to Langerwehe and Frenzerberg Castle. Here men of the 9th Infantry prepare to move out over a berm as the tanks move forward.

Tanks of the 3rd Battalion, 32nd Armored, Task Force Richardson move out under enemy artillery fire through muddy fields to Hücheln on 25 November. Between the two medium tank companies, more than twelve tanks were lost to mines and/or were stuck in mud and had to be pulled out by recovery vehicles.

A continuation of the action from above as the tank column continues to advance under heavy fire. The caption states that in the distance an American tank is burning after being hit. Note the bright panels on each tank for identification to friendly aircraft.

More scenes from the action around Hücheln. The area was bordered by a railroad on one side and a town with factory area on the other. Smoke has been laid to help shield the armored advance.

Away from the advance of the main thrust of the medium tank companies around Hücheln, an M36 90mm GMC moves up with infantrymen on 25 November.

Wonderful ground-level image of GIs from the 2nd Battalion, 47th Infantry Regiment with 3rd Armored tank support moving through Hücheln on the first day of the assault in the area. Tanks and tank destroyers can be seen in the background.

A break in the action shows a column of light tanks of Company C, 3rd Battalion, 32nd Armored Regiment lining a street in Hücheln on 25 November.

A great photo that shows ten M4 medium tanks of Task Force Richardson continuing their advance around Hücheln on 25 November. The open muddy fields gave the Germans an excellent field of fire and offered minimal cover for the supporting infantry.

After the battles at Hastenrath in November 1944, men from Company F, 33rd Armored Regiment inspect a tank knocked out in the area. Based on the registration number we know this tank was lost on 16 November. The soldier in the driver's hatch is Private Arthur Ecklund and he would be killed in action at Stoumont, Belgium on 20 December as the Battle of the Bulge was getting into full swing.

An M5A1 light tank of the 33rd Armored Regiment that has seen better days is being hoisted onto a trailer by an armored recovery vehicle near Mausbach on 29 November. The tank was probably pulled from the battlefield and will be worked on. Note the rail around the turret, almost certainly a field model.

135

On 9 December, the 703rd Tank Destroyer Battalion performed firing tests from their 90mm guns against a German Panther from the 116th Panzer Division outside of Stolberg. Numerous shots were fired and recorded, as evidenced by the numbered markings in various spots on the tank.

On 10 December, Task Force Hogan from the 33rd Armored Regiment and Task Force Kane from the 32nd Armored Regiment initiated actions to take the towns of Obergeich, Geich, Echtz and Hoven to further the 3rd Armored lines from the Langerwehe area. Tanks from the 738th Tank Battalion were supplied to help with mine-clearing and here is an M32 ARV pushing a T1E1 Earthworm mine-exploder outside of Langerwehe on the first day of the action.

One of the most well-known photos of the Second World War is of two GIs from the 3rd Armored Division sitting behind an M4 medium tank looking cold, nervous and anticipating their next move. The photo was taken 11 December in Geich, Germany and this photo was taken from another angle and shows one of those soldiers with a Thompson SMG, now joined by two riflemen of the 36th Armored Infantry Regiment.

GIs of Company B, 1st Battalion, 60th Infantry Regiment of the 9th Infantry Division who were supporting the 3rd Armored in these December actions move through Langerwehe on 10 December towards the front lines at Geich and Obergeich.

Tanks of Task Force Hogan approach the outskirts of Obergeich on 10 December with infantry supporting them. In the distance a tank has either been hit by a mine or anti-tank fire as it approached the entrance to the town.

Staff Sergeant Cecil Smitherman from Headquarters Company, 1st Battalion, 32nd Armored Regiment, Task Force Kane receives coordinates for an artillery barrage outside of Echtz on 10 December.

Sergeant Sylvester Weir of Berlin, Wisconsin, a GI from the 36th Armored Infantry Regiment, checks out a destroyed building in Langerwehe on 10 December.

Surely a posed photograph, but nonetheless a great image of a 'Blitzdough' of the 36th Armored Infantry in Langerwehe. Private First Class Edward Manfred of Brooklyn, New York peers through an 'open window' in the village on 10 December.

A T1E3 'Aunt Jemima' supporting the 3rd Armored Division near Langerwehe has become stuck in a muddy ditch on 11 December. The photographer stated that this tank was with the 33rd Armored Regiment, but more likely was from the 738th Tank Battalion (Special) which was providing mine-clearing tanks to the division.

Tanks of Task Force Kane, 1st Battalion, 32nd Armored Regiment enter the shell-torn town of Echtz after finally clearing it on 11 December.

GIs move through Obergeich after finally taking the town on 11 December. A half-track from Company B, 36th Armored Infantry Regiment moves past down the war-torn and muddy streets of the town.

Further past Obergeich, GIs and a half-track of the 3rd Armored Division move into the next objective of Geich on 11 December.

Private First Class Walter Siarkowski (who would be KIA in late December in the Ardennes) and Sergeant Leonard Abraham, both of Company G, 33rd Armored Regiment examine a knocked-out German StuG III Ausf.G outside Obergeich on 11 December.

The two soldiers from the previous photo were photographed on their tank pointing to the town of Geich after posing for the first picture. The vehicle is an M4A1 (76) medium tank.

An American M5A1 light tank moves past a German roadblock of knocked-down logs and a dead German soldier in Echtz on 12 December. Following behind the light tank is an M4 medium tank.

Medics with the 32nd Armored Regiment load a wounded soldier into a medical half-track in Echtz on 12 December. Again, the muddy conditions facing the troops at this time are evident in the photo.

On the outskirts of Echtz, the signal corps cameraman photographed a dead American soldier from either the 3rd Armored or 9th Infantry Division before being removed by the graves registration team.

A GI from the
9th Infantry or
3rd Armored
with two of the
young German
prisoners tasked
with defending the
Geich and Echtz
area. Luckily for
them, the war is
over.

A photograph
taken just before
the 33rd Armored
Regiment
moved out to
the Ardennes to
stem the German
offensive. This
M5A1 light
tank belongs to
Company C, Task
Force Hogan.

CHAPTER THREE

The 3rd Armored Division would be directed back to Belgium to meet the German offensive, right in the area where the German 5th Panzer and 6th Waffen SS Panzer armies' attacks were taking place. One by one, units of CCA, CCB and CCR were given orders and making the mad dash back to Belgium. In the Ardennes the 3rd Armored would face some of the best German divisions: the 1st, 2nd and 9th SS Panzer Divisions and the 116th Panzer Division. Numerous books have been written about the Battle of the Bulge, so what follows will just be a summary of the highlights involving the 3rd Armored Division during the Bulge battles.

CCA moved out first, arrived in the Eupen area on 18 December and was assigned to the V Corps sector to help. Here they remained in reserve until units were moving to the area of Grandménil and Marche on 21 December. CCB was the next to arrive and they headed to the XVIII Airborne Corps sector around La Gleize and Stavelot to assist there. The 30th Infantry Division was already heavily engaged here with the 1st SS Panzer Division and desperately needed armored support. The infamous Joachim Peiper and his Kampfgruppe were battling the 30th Infantry at this time. CCB consisted of Task Force Welborn and Lovelady and they quickly deployed into roadblocks. Task Force Welborn was broken down into two smaller forces, McGeorge and Jordan, and they were working hand in hand with the 30th Infantry Division. While Lovelady was busy around Trois-Ponts and Grand Coo, Task Force Jordan headed to Stoumont, while McGeorge began to face stiff resistance near La Gleize where Kampfgruppe Peiper had entrenched themselves. Task Force Jordan, attached to the 119th Infantry Regiment of the 30th Infantry Division, was approaching La Gleize from the west while Task Force McGeorge moved in from the east. By 24 December the surrounded Germans abandoned the town, leaving their dead, wounded and vehicles for the 3rd Armored task forces. In addition to twenty-six tanks taken by the Americans, there were numerous other armored vehicles and artillery pieces in addition to a few hundred prisoners that the 3rd Armored captured. By Christmas Day, the task forces had rejoined CCB near Spa for a brief rest.

While CCB was engaged against the 1st SS Panzer Division, CCR was addressing several threats in their general area. In order to meet these different threats, CCR was broke into several smaller task forces. The bulk of the CCR and other divisional units reached the area of Hotton and Manhay on 19 December. Task Force Orr was given the areas around Amonines, Dochamps and Samrée,

Task Force Hogan would move to the River Ourthe, and Task Force Kane set roadblocks near Manhay and Dochamps. In essence, Kane had the left, Orr the center and Hogan the right. Task Force Orr quickly found themselves in bitter action around Amonines and Samrée where Company H, 33rd Armored Regiment would lose most of their tanks. Task Force Hogan at Beffe was being attacked from the north and south-east, and quickly found themselves surrounded at Marcouray. This task force would soon be known as 'Hogan's 400'.

There was a mixed force in Hotton of men from the 143rd Signal Company, a small group from Task Force Kane, a light tank company from the 33rd Armored Regiment and various divisional and engineer units that would be forced to defend the town from the main thrust of the 116th Panzer Division. The German tanks attacked Hotton ferociously, but the stubborn mixed bag of Spearhead defenders would not budge and the Germans gave up their attack by 23 December. Meanwhile, Task Force Hogan was still surrounded and attempts made to resupply the troops with medical supplies by firing them from artillery did not work out. Hogan was ordered to leave his serious wounded, disable his vehicles and make his way back to friendly lines. With their faces blackened, and tired and hungry, the men of Hogan's 400 arrived back at Soy on 26 December. CCB relieved CCR around this time for a much-needed rest and refit.

Just as this sector was getting under control somewhat, the German 2nd SS Panzer Division was thrusting towards Manhay and Grandménil. Task Force Richardson of CCA was moved to this area on 21 December to help Task Force Kane. The Germans took Odeigne and battered Task Force Richardson at Freyneux on 23-24 December before taking Manhay and Grandménil on the 24th and 25th. However, they were stopped at Oster on Christmas Day. The 7th Armored Division came to help the 3rd Armored at this time in Manhay and by 26 December, the Germans were kicked out of Grandménil and Manhay. Tank wrecks from both sides littered the small villages. By Christmas Day, Task Force McGeorge of CCB moved in to replace the battered units of Task Force Kane and Richardson. In addition to the 7th Armored coming to help bolster the defenses in the area, the 75th Infantry Division arrived as well for infantry support. A brief but brutal battle flared up at Sadzot when the 12th SS Panzer Division attempted to exploit a gap between the 75th Infantry and Task Force Orr lines near Sadzot. The American 509th Parachute Battalion was instrumental in turning back this attack that raged throughout the night.

The period from 28 December through New Year's Day 1945 until 3 January allowed the 3rd Armored to rest and refit again. The now cold and blustery weather was unwelcome as trench foot and frostbite struck those soldiers not fortunate enough to have warm homes in which to bunk. Tanks and other vehicles were covered in snow and took longer to start up each day. By 3 January though,

VII Corps was ready for the next phase of the Battle of the Bulge. Now that the German offensive had been stopped, it was time for the Americans to go on the offensive and push the enemy back to Germany. The 2nd Armored Division with the 84th Infantry Division would move on one flank, while the 3rd Armored with the 83rd Infantry Division attached would move on the other. The objective was to close up at Houffalize. The battles in the deep frigid snow would be characterized by small but vicious engagements centered around small Belgian villages.

On 3 January, Task Force Lovelady moved towards Malempré, Task Force McGeorge headed to Jevigné and into Banneux, while Task Force Richardson moved to Lanisval and Task Force Hogan was past Manhay to secure the crossroads. The Germans were literally being pushed out of each Belgian village one by one. Tanks and vehicles not knocked out by enemy fire fell prey to the icy and snowy roads. By 6 January CCA had moved into Grand-Sart and Hébronval, while CCB moved on Règné and Bihain. Welborn and Lovelady battled at Ottré and Hogan moved to Règné after being relieved. After six days of brutal combat, by 9 January the 3rd Armored had won 11km of frozen ground. One thing that was becoming even more apparent to the men of the division, despite their success, was that the M4 medium tank was no match for the German Panther. The veterans of the division wanted more armor and an improved gun to battle the Germans. Many of the men let their displeasure be known to the various press reporters always hanging around. The 3rd Armored paused on 9 January to let the 83rd Infantry push through and establish a bridgehead on a line of Bovigny to Bâclain to Mont-le-Ban. By the time the 3rd Armored was ready to start back up on 13 January, that line had not fully been reached.

CCB was given the lead to exploit the bridgehead towards Bâclain and on to Vaux and Sterpigny, while CCA guarded the left flank and CCR was held in reserve. Task Force Lovelady attacked from Langlir to Lomré and by 14 January Task Force Walker (Welborn) maneuvered through a minefield near Bâclain before taking the town. Lovelady bypassed Mont-le-Ban and was 1,000 yards short of Cherain, while elements of CCR, Task Forces Kane and Hogan took Mont-le-Ban. The next battles the 3rd Armored Division would encounter would be some of the fiercest, and in reading veterans' memoirs, the cause of some of the bitterest memories from the war. CCB was aiming to force the Germans out of Cherain and Sterpigny where the 9th SS Panzer Division was still holding with other German Army units. On 15-16 January, Task Force Lovelady lost all of their medium tanks in the attack on Cherain. Tanks from CCA had to be called up to quickly fill the ranks of CCB. Meanwhile, Task Force Welborn with Kane and Richardson in support was also getting its bell rung at Sterpigny. Numerous tanks littered the fields outside the town and also inside the village. Finally, by 18 January the areas had been cleared but not until after heavy tank losses.

However, the end was in sight for the German Ardennes offensive. Units began retreating en masse to the German border. Once Houffalize was reached, the Germans west of it had been cut off and defeated. The 4th Cavalry Group would replace the 3rd Armored Division in the line. After a few weeks resting in Belgium, the division would return to their old home around Stolberg. Replacements were needed for tank crews and officers, pretty much at every level. The survivors of the Bulge were bitter over the performance of the M4 tank and demanded something bigger and better. They would receive ten of the new T26E3 Pershing tanks with a 90mm gun, but ten was not enough. They knew the end was in sight for the German Army and all that was needed was a final push, but no one wanted to die this close to the end of the war. The veterans knew too that these last few battles on German soil with the German soldiers having their backs against the wall would be brutal. The men of the Spearhead left the Ardennes cold, tired and battered, yet still victorious. They took the time in late January and most of February to rest and get their vehicles up to full operating condition. They prepared themselves for the jump across the River Roer and the Rhine and then into the heart of Germany. The Spearhead was about to make its final move.

An M5A1 light tank from Task Force Kane in a roadblock position outside Manhay, Belgium on 23 December. Elements of the 2nd SS Panzer Division were headed towards the area and intense fighting would occur shortly. Note the bundles of straw added for camouflage in addition to the boards in front.

Another tank of Task Force Kane in roadblock position near the M5A1 from above, this time an M4A1. The roadblocks would be overrun by the tanks of the 2nd SS Panzer Division on 23 December.

Two tankers with Company I, 32nd Armored Regiment, Corporal Henry Ferraro and T/5 Alfred Mahoney, camouflage their tank near Hotton, Belgium on 26 December. Hotton was the scene of fierce fighting just days before this photo was taken.

Members of the 3rd Armored Division inspect a German Mark V Panther of the 116th Panzer Division knocked out in the Hotton fighting. It was knocked out in a garden behind the Rue Haute in Hotton on 21 December.

Lieutenant John Modrak of Company C, 33rd Armored Regiment inspects a knocked-out M4 medium tank from Company G, 32nd Armored Regiment in Hotton on 26 December. The caption indicated that the tank had been used by the Germans, but local historian Dieter Laes has confirmed that the tank was not used by the Germans at all but was in fact knocked out by them in the battle for Hotton.

Not too far away from the photo above, Lieutenant Modrak inspects an Sd.Kfz.251 German half-track and a Panzer IV tank with tactical number '602' close by. Both vehicles are from the 116th Panzer Division.

Yet another photo of Lieutenant Modrak and his men inspecting knocked-out German armor in and around Hotton. Cameraman Harold Roberts was obviously following them around town. Here Modrak and his men check out a Panther Ausf.F and a Panzer IV '611' in Hotton on 26 December.

A common scene in the early days of the Ardennes offensive: Belgian civilians fleeing their towns as the battle raged. Here civilians pass a 3rd Armored Division tank on their way from Trou de Bra, Belgium on 26 December.

A soldier with the 3rd Armored gets to know a small Belgian child sitting on his M3A1 half-track in the town of Soy where Colonel Sam Hogan's 'Lost 400' were about to return to friendly lines after being cut off for a few days.

With their faces still blackened from the nighttime escape to friendly lines, men of Task Force Hogan enjoy rations and cigarettes in a courtyard of a church in Soy on 26 December.

Second Lieutenant Texas Barnes of the 54th Armored Field Artillery Battalion eats some rations upon his return to his own lines at Soy. Battery C of the 54th was one of the units that comprised Task Force Hogan.

Two more men from the 54th Armored Field Artillery Battalion, Corporal James Sweetman and Private Edward Mattos, rest after their return to safety. Mattos would be wounded at Büsbach on 2 March 1945.

Three men of the 83rd Armored Reconnaissance Battalion – Private James Day, Second Lieutenant Robert Ricketts and Corporal Stanley Micolowski – enjoy some lighthearted moments after returning to safety.

Private Floyd Carlson of the 83rd Armored Reconnaissance Battalion spreads butter and jelly on toast after his safe return. The men of Task Force Hogan were low on ammo, food and other supplies during the time behind enemy lines.

Private First Class Clarence Collins, a tanker with G Company, 33rd Armored Regiment, enjoys some rations after a grueling night march to return to safety.

Private James Houston of the 54th Armored Field Artillery Battalion, his face still blackened from the night march, takes a load off with his trusty Thompson SMG propped up on his leg.

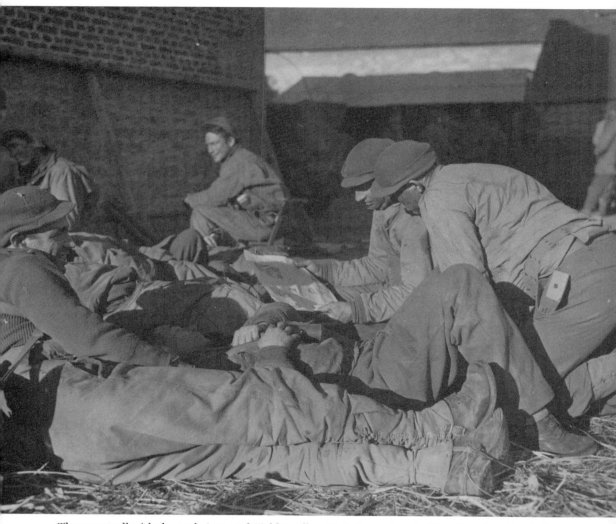

Three men all with the 54th Armored Field Artillery Battalion – Private First Class Ray Paschall, Private Jesse Miller and T/5 Robert Kelley – take the time to rest and catch up on the news after being behind enemy lines for the past several days.

While two comrades bask in the December sun on the church roof in Soy, Private Billie Utz, a medic with the 83rd Armored Reconnaissance Battalion, rests and prepares to dig into his rations.

Another group of 83rd Armored Reconnaissance Battalion men joke and relax in the courtyard in Soy. After their last few days of being cut off and surrounded, the mood of the men was one of good spirits and relief.

Great photo of a grizzled NCO of the 3rd Armored Division at this time. Sergeant James Smith of the 54th Armored Field Artillery Battalion enjoys a cigar after his escape with Task Force Hogan.

Private Herbert Edwards of the 54th Armored Field Artillery Battalion relaxes with others of the 'lost unit' at Soy.

Private Charles Keeton of the 83rd Armored Reconnaissance Battalion stretches outs, while other members of the 'lost unit' mill about the courtyard and share their stories with one another.

Pictured here in the middle of his meal is tank platoon leader with Company G, 33rd Armored Regiment, Lieutenant Fred Matzenbacher.

T/5 Herman Rewerts (KIA, April 1945) and Private John Mulee, both of Headquarters Company, 3rd Battalion, 33rd Armored Regiment, Task Force Hogan, enjoy their smokes after returning to friendly lines on 26 December.

After beating back the Germans around the Hotten area, it was time for defenses to be shored up. Here, men of the 23rd Armored Engineer Battalion move concertina wire in the fields around Hotton on 28 December.

Nearby the above photo, engineers were also digging emplacements for tanks. Here, an M4 medium tank of Task Force Lovelady, 33rd Armored Regiment moves into a newly-dug position for better concealment and protection.

Sergeant Tony Stozer with the 23rd Armored Engineer Battalion keeps an alert eye toward the enemy in front of a well-camouflaged tank with his .30 caliber light machine gun. The photograph was taken with the previous two ones on 28 December outside Hotton.

This particular army cameraman had a good sense of humor in taking this shot. A black cat sits atop a German Panther tank in the village of Hotton on 28 December after it was knocked out by the 3rd Armored Division.

A column of vehicles stands ready to move out when the orders are received in Soy, Belgium on 27 December.

M4 medium tanks and half-tracks of the 2nd Battalion, 32nd Armored Regiment move out near Marche, Belgium on 31 December. Snow has begun to fall; the 3rd Armored has not whitewashed any vehicles yet but rather still have the foliage applied as camouflage.

A German Panther from the 2nd SS Panzer Division knocked out at an intersection on the road between Manhay and Grandménil during their attack on the 3rd Armored Division on 23 December.

This Panther also from the 2nd SS Panzer Division was knocked out in the town of Grandménil by elements of Task Force McGeorge and paratroopers of the 517th Parachute Infantry on 26 December. The 75th Infantry Division would move into the town on the 30th.

Under a camouflage net, soldiers with the 23rd Armored Engineer Battalion change tires and rims next to a half-track near the town of Wéris on 30 December.

Medics from the 32nd Armored Regiment look at their jeep after it was damaged in the brutal fighting at Sadzot, Belgium on 27 December. Note the roll of barbed wire on the rear of the vehicle in the foreground.

Photo of a German tank captured at Hotton, but destroyed to prevent its re-use by the Germans and also for cinematic effect as the scene was also filmed by the motion picture men attached to the 3rd Armored in this area in late December.

Hot chow has been brought out from the rear to the front lines for a New Year's Eve turkey dinner for these men of the 2nd Battalion, 32nd Armored Regiment near Marche, Belgium on 31 December.

M4 (105) assault guns from the 32nd Armored Regiment, CCA provide fire support near Trou de Bra, Belgium on 3 January.

Another angle of the photo above, showing the stacks of 105mm shells that the assault guns are using in their fire support. The half-track seems to be in a role of ammunition carrier for the tanks.

Yet another photo of the fire support team in action, now with an M7 105mm Howitzer Motor Carriage visible in front of the M4 (105) assault guns. A trailer with 105mm shells is behind the M7 in the foreground.

The 82nd Airborne Division infantrymen ride into Trou de Bra, Belgium on an M4A3E2 (75) 'Jumbo'. The signal corps cameraman Peter Petrony, who took the previous photos of 105mm assault guns firing on German positions outside of the village, must have returned to the town as additional units were moving in.

One last shot of the fire support team in the field outside Trou de Bra. Note the hills surrounding the area, typical of this area of the Ardennes in Belgium.

An M4 medium tank crew from Company F, 2nd Battalion, 32nd Armored Regiment heads back to the rear after their tank was knocked out by a German anti-tank gun near Floret on 1 January.

Major General Maurice Rose confers with Brigadier General Doyle Hickey on a wooded trail in the Ardennes as CCA of the 3rd Armored advances towards the German lines. Note the censor's marks on the map that Hickey is holding. The jeep driver has a Thompson SMG in a leather scabbard attached to the jeep.

T/5 Harold Roberts of the 165th Signal Photographic Company was attached to the 3rd Armored Division normally and he took many of the photos in this book. Here he is photographed in front of a Panther tank seen previously, but now with snow. This is the 2nd SS Panzer Division tank knocked out at the intersection near Grandménil.

George Bloth of the 83rd Armored Reconnaissance Battalion took a few photos during the Ardennes battles. Here is an M4A2 medium tank of the 3rd Armored in a yard outside a Belgian farmhouse. This was a British M4 that was among hundreds that were loaned to the Americans to make up for the tank losses early in the Bulge battles. Note the contrast in the olive drab tank next to the white snow. (© *George H. Bloth Collection*)

Another abandoned German sWS. It has a camouflage tarp over the rear to provide protection for the supplies and men it was transporting. (© *George H. Bloth Collection*)

A German Schwerer Wehrmachtsschlepper mit Pritschenaufbau (sWS) lies abandoned off a road somewhere in Belgium during the Ardennes offensive. (© *George H. Bloth Collection*)

An M5A1 light tank standing guard on roadblock duty somewhere in the Ardennes in January 1945. The tank has the unique bracket near the bow gunner's machine gun, typical of the 33rd Armored Regiment tanks.

In the woods is pictured an M4A1 (76) and an M4A3E2 Jumbo assault tank of the 3rd Armored Division. The crews grab a quick smoke as they await their next move.

A dead German soldier lays propped up in a wheelbarrow of sorts next to an M5A1 light tank in Banneux on 5 January. The light tank appears to have had the number 15 applied on it at one time and it also sports a lucky shamrock on the side.

Another dead German soldier in the Banneux area. The 1st Battalion, 33rd Armored Regiment was in the area of Banneux at this time.

An M4A3 (75) medium tank of the 1st Battalion, 33rd Armored Regiment attempts to navigate the icy terrain in Banneux on 5 January. There is also movie footage of this exact scene and the tank was in fact having difficulty navigating this slight rise in terrain.

A tank of the 3rd Armored in the Malempré area on 5 January prepares to pass an abandoned and snow-covered German Panther that has been pushed to the roadside.

Another German Panther that has been pushed off the road near Malempré, taken just after the photo above by cameraman Harold Roberts.

An M36 90mm Gun Motor Carriage of the 703rd Tank Destroyer Battalion leads a column down a wooded road near Malempré, Belgium on 5 January.

Series of three photos that show the attempts to pull out a stuck M36 of the 703rd Tank Destroyer Battalion near Manhay on 4 January. The vehicle is with Company B of the 703rd.

Chains and cables are being attached to the front so that the M36 can be pulled out by an armored recovery vehicle.

Success has been realized as the M36 is pulled from the ditch and can now be put back in the line for action against the Germans near Manhay.

An M4A3E2 assault gun of Company G, 33rd Armored Regiment, Task Force Hogan moves towards the front lines from Manhay on 4 January. By this time, the 83rd Infantry Division was attached to various 3rd Armored units for extra infantry support and the GIs on this tank are from Company A, 1st Battalion, 330th Infantry Regiment.

A young Waffen SS soldier who has been wounded lies on the hood of a jeep to be transported back behind the lines by the Americans. Note the camouflage tunic he wears, typical of the SS at this time.

A bulldozer with the 49th Combat Engineer Battalion pushes a German Panther tank that was blocking the Manhay–Vaux-Chavanne road on 6 January.

M4 medium tanks of the 3rd Armored advance cautiously through a snow-covered road in the Ardennes forest. Guns are pointed towards potential enemy positions. The location is the Manhay-Houffalize road near Fraiture on 7 January.

Further down the road from the previous photo, engineers with the 23rd Armored Engineer Battalion sweep for mines near Fraiture, Belgium. According to the caption, the tank in the background was knocked out by enemy mines.

Crew of an M4 medium tank from the 3rd Armored Division warm themselves with a tarp-covered shelter and stove. The conditions at this time were freezing, so any warm shelter was welcome and given the smiles of the men, the warmth and hot coffee were quite welcome. The tank has duckbill extenders applied to the tracks for dealing with the slippery conditions.

An artillery position of M7 105mm HMCs in a snow-covered field in Belgium. Camouflage netting covers the vehicles for extra protection from enemy spotters.

A snow-covered road near Houffalize has caused an M5A1 light tank of the 3rd Armored Division to skid into a ditch. It is being towed out by an M31 Armored Recovery Vehicle.

Further down the road from the previous photo, on 9 January a jeep passes a knocked-out
German Panther near Houffalize. The tank is most likely from the 9th SS Panzer Division.

A column of M5A1 light tanks from the 3rd Armored moves into Sart, Belgium on 9 January. As the 3rd Armored pushed back the stubborn German units, Belgian towns were being retaken every few days.

A column of 3rd Armored and 83rd Infantry Division vehicles make their way through Lierneux on 9 January.

This photo was taken at the exact same spot as above, but now an M4A3E2 can be seen moving past GIs of the 331st Infantry Regiment, 83rd Infantry. The snow that has fallen on the vehicle provides a natural camouflage.

Based on close examination, this M4A3E2 'Jumbo' appears to be a different one to that featured in the previous photo. Based on where some of the snow is on each vehicle, they appear to be different tanks.

Another view of the movement on the streets of Lierneux on 9 January. Here GIs from the 83rd move past an M4 medium tank 'F-11'.

Still in Lierneux, a military policeman directs traffic on the busy streets. An armored recovery vehicle named 'Ball-Breaker' is moving past as the MP stares at the cameraman.

January 10 and the German tanks knocked out in Hotton are still visible in their original locations. This aerial photo shows the Panther and Panzer IV that were seen in previous photos at the beginning of the Ardennes battles.

Harold Roberts continued to take photos from an L-4 Piper Cub and here around Hotton he found two German Jagdpanzer assault guns in the woods that had been knocked out.

A column of 3rd Armored vehicles moves into another Belgian town after pushing out the German defenders. A dead German soldier who seems to have been frozen in place lies on the village outskirts.

On 10 January a soldier from the 84th Infantry Division inspects an M7 105mm HMC left by Task Force Hogan in December 1944 in Marcouray. The vehicle is named 'Cadillac', making it from Battery C of the 54th Armored Field Battalion and it still has its hedgerow-cutters on the front from the Normandy campaigns.

Also in Marcouray, taken in the same photo sequence as above, a GI inspects the remains of a half-track, also left abandoned by Task Force Hogan in December. Prior to making their way back to friendly lines by foot, the men of Task Force Hogan rendered all their vehicles inoperable so as to prevent their use by the Germans.

Soldiers of the 3rd Armored Division move past three M5A1 light tanks with an M4 medium tank in the background around Langlir, Belgium on 13 January.

Another photo of Langlir on 13 January showing a vehicular column of the 3rd Armored and attached 83rd Infantry Division troops moving through the town and, according to the caption, under enemy shell-fire at the time.

Langlir was the scene of intense fighting for the men of the Spearhead and their comrades in the 83rd Infantry. Here a soldier peers out from the cover of a light tank as enemy shells land in and around Langlir on 13 January.

Another photo from Langlir showing a section of road that has been zeroed in by German artillery. A weapons carrier and half-track lie smoldering from artillery hits by the enemy.

Another view of the area in the previous photo, but from a different angle. Here a jeep races past the half-track and also an M4 medium tank from Company F, 33rd Armored Regiment, making it a vehicle from Task Force Welborn, CCB.

The action around this area in Langlir on 13 January was intense and signal corps' photographer Harold Roberts continued to snap away. Here he captured a soldier running past the same half-track and M4 medium tank shown above.

The last photo taken at the road in Langlir featured in the previous few photos. Here, Private Thomas Amenta of Los Angeles, CA walks back to the rear after his tank had been knocked out by a mine just outside Langlir on 13 January. Amenta was with Company I, 33rd Armored Regiment, the other medium tank company of Task Force Welborn.

An M5A1 light tank moves up a street in Langlir towards the German lines on 13 January.

An M36 90mm GMC of the 703rd Tank Destroyer Battalion moves past a knocked-out German Panzer IV outside Langlir, Belgium on 13 January. There is movie footage of this exact scene taken by a signal corps' cameraman who was riding in and filming from an M5A1 light tank.

421456

Taken on the same road as above, an M4 medium tank leads a column out of Langlir towards the enemy lines on 13 January.

Panther number '121' from the 9th SS Panzer Division was knocked out by the anti-tank units of the 331st Infantry Regiment, attached to the 3rd Armored Division in front of a house on the outskirts of Langlir on 13 January. Note the panzerfaust on the engine deck.

Up close image of the Panther above, showing the armor-piercing hole just under the turret numbers.

A knocked-out American jeep sits silent in Langlir on 13 January. The caption stated that the dog in the driver's seat was in fact the pet of a German soldier who had been killed in action.

German prisoners captured in and around Langlir on 13 January are prepared to be moved to the rear. They are in the rear of the truck guarded by a lone GI.

Military policemen and other soldiers from the 3rd Armored watch German prisoners captured in Ottré on 14 January being lined up for processing and shipment back to the rear.

Another photo of the PoWs above, this time from the front. This photo clearly shows the SS tunic on one soldier and also the camouflage pants that the Waffen SS used at this time.

Two GIs of the 36th Armored Infantry Regiment stand guard in their trench position in the snowy landscape of the Ardennes. They have a bazooka within reach to counter any armored vehicles that may approach.

Captain Joe Robertson congratulates his commander of the 83rd Armored Reconnaissance Battalion, Lieutenant Colonel Prentice Yeomans on receiving the Bronze Star Medal in Bihain on 14 January. Yeoman would be killed in action near the end of the war in April 1945.

Wrecked German equipment litters the road in the path to the front-line town of Montleban on 15 January.

A Belgian house catches fire after American troops attempted to build a fire to warm themselves. Here GIs are assisting in the evacuation of the house.

In the rear lines around 15 January, an M4A3 (75) medium tank of the 3rd Armored Division sports a fresh whitewash paint job. In addition to the whitewash, the tank also has duckbill extenders on the T54E2 steel tracks for extra traction.

An M4A1 (76) follows an M4A3E2 'Jumbo' through the town of Lomré on 16 January. These tanks are with Task Force Lovelady of the 33rd Armored Regiment.

The cameraman who took many of these photos, Harold Roberts, is photographed again, this time after receiving a slight shrapnel wound to his head. Roberts is standing in front of an M31 Armored Recovery Vehicle and is wearing an Army Air Force bomber jacket he traded for and that his family still has today. Lomré, Belgium, 16 January.

An M8 Armored Car is pulled out of an embankment by an M3A1 half-track outside Lomré on 16 January.

Whitewashed M4 (105) assault guns of the 3rd Armored blend with the snow to make difficult targets for German armor in the 75th Infantry Division sector of the Ardennes on 16 January.

A direct hit on an M7 105mm HMC of the 54th Armored Field Artillery Battalion outside a Belgian village. Various ammunition trailers are placed at different locations around the battery's firing area.

Tanks and other armored vehicles parked in Cherain before making the next assault on the area. The fighting around Cherain and Sterpigny resulted in heavy tank losses for the 3rd Armored Division. The circular sign on the tree in the foreground says 'Oriole', the code name for the 32nd Armored Regiment.

A knocked-out M4A1 (76) sits on a street in Cherain on 17 January. It appears that a maintenance or ordnance unit has marked the tank 'repl', meaning 'needing replacement'.

Litter-bearers of a 3rd Armored Division medical team pick up two soldiers of their unit whose truck was hit by German shellfire at Sterpigny on 20 January.

GIs inspect a German artillery piece in a Belgian field near the end of the Ardennes offensive. The retreating Germans left numerous artillery pieces and vehicles strewn about in their retreat to Germany.

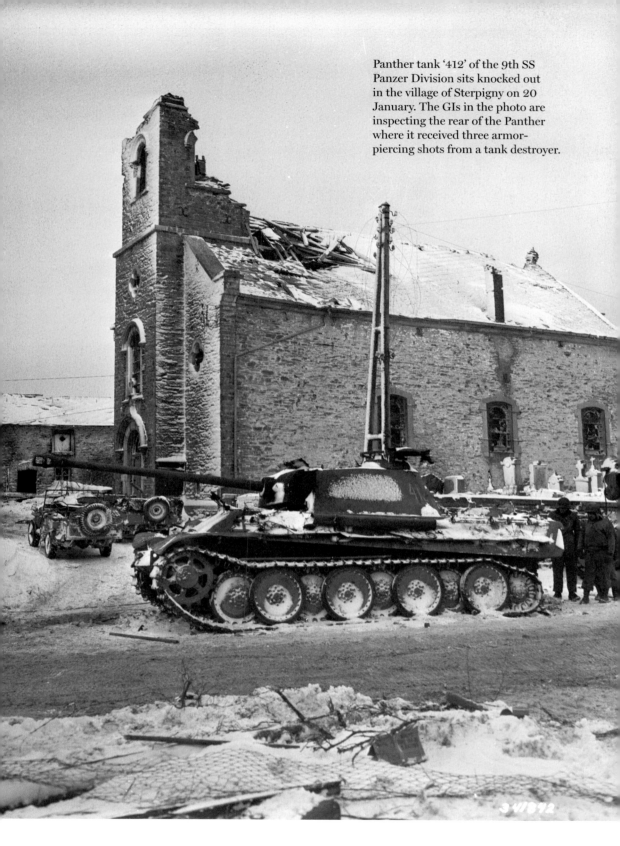

Panther tank '412' of the 9th SS Panzer Division sits knocked out in the village of Sterpigny on 20 January. The GIs in the photo are inspecting the rear of the Panther where it received three armor-piercing shots from a tank destroyer.

3 4/1872

Captain Hollis Towne of the 3rd Battalion, 32nd Armored Regiment inspects a knocked-out M4A1 (76) in Sterpigny. The lower transmission cover still has the remaining parts of a hedgerow-cutter from the Normandy action. Captain Towne would be killed in action on 15 April 1945.

A German Panther of the 9th SS Panzer Division lays knocked out outside Sart-Lez-St. Vith (Rodt) Belgium on 23 January. An armor-piercing round has penetrated the lower front corner of the turret, blowing off a chunk of armor, and another has penetrated the lower turret side.

CHAPTER FOUR

The 3rd Armored Division returned to the Stolberg area of Germany on 7 February after spending the last two months in Belgium. Replacements streamed in to fill the ranks of the tank crews, infantry squads and other units. While the division would still field some 75mm medium tanks, up-gunned 76mm models began to fill out the companies. A welcome addition of ten T26E3 'Pershing' tanks was added to the ranks as well with their powerful 90mm gun. Finally the men had a tank that could take on the German Panther and Tiger one-on-one. Tank crews were given the chance to showcase the test-firing of the new tanks at Gressenich in late February to a collection of high-ranking generals including Major General Maurice Rose and Lieutenant General Courtney Hodges of the US First Army. The River Roer was to be the jumping-off point for the offensive into Germany. While the division finalized their rest and refitting period, the 8th and 104th Infantry divisions would force crossings over the Roer at Duren on 23 February. The 3rd Armored would pass through this bridgehead after the infantry divisions cleared the area. Spearhead would then attack through Blatzheim, Kerpen, Manheim and Buir, then cross the Erft Canal area before moving on towards the prize of Cologne on the Rhine.

On 26 February, the task forces of the 3rd Armored jumped off with their assault. Quickly the soldiers realized that the latest attack into the heartland of Germany would be different from the battles of the Westwall. There were no dragons' teeth and concrete bunkers here, but rather roadblocks made out of timber logs, and roaming panzerfaust teams of one or two soldiers, many young or old. The division didn't meet any Volksturm (people's militia) in the fall of 1944 but now they did. CCA was deployed on the right of the bridgehead and CCB was on the left. Task Force Kane and the 83rd Armored Reconnaissance Battalion took Buir on the first day and then proceeded to Manheim. The action on the right and the center was the most intense. Task Force Miller, comprising the 2nd Battalion, 32nd Armored Regiment, met the toughest resistance in their area. Starting with roadblocks in Golzheim, the task force took a beating on their attack to Blatzheim and then on to Bergenhausen, losing several tanks in a matter of hours. By 27 February though, the task force took Kerpen on the Erft Canal and was only 9 miles from Cologne.

Meanwhile, CCB with Task Forces Lovelady and Welborn were headed to Elsdorf with Welborn in the lead. Elsdorf would be the scene of the first Pershing that was knocked out by enemy action. 'Fireball', a Pershing with Company F, 1st Battalion, 33rd Armored Regiment of Task Force Welborn was knocked out on 27 February by a German Tiger 1 tank, resulting in the death of two tankers. However, on the next day revenge was doled out by a Pershing from Task Force Lovelady that had moved into Elsdorf to support Welborn. Sergeant Nicholas Mashlonik and his Pershing crew not only knocked out a German Tiger 1 of the same unit that hit 'Fireball' but also two German Panzer IV tanks outside the city. The Erft Canal was the last barrier before the land opened up to Cologne. Task Force Richardson from the 32nd Armored and Task Force Hogan from the 33rd Armored were given the Erft Canal area to clear at Paffendorf and Glesch respectively. Both towns were taken with quick action and the Erft bridgehead was expanded on 28 February. Supporting the division during this time was the 395th Infantry Regiment from the 99th Infantry Division and the 4th Cavalry Group. With the bridgehead secured, the 3rd Armored fanned out for the race to Cologne.

Spearhead continued their advance to Cologne in early March. Towns with roadblocks and small elements of armor here and there were the typical encounters. The German Army in the west was in a shambles and the armor that they could throw at the Americans was limited, usually consisting of one or two assault guns and minimal medium and heavy tank support. The division moved through towns such as Pulheim, Sinthern, Roggendorf and Niederhausen on their way to Cologne. Along the way the roadblocks were dealt with and once again the ground-to-air coordination with the fighter bombers proved crucial in the rapid advance by the division. By 5 March the great city of Cologne on the Rhine was in sight as the units spread out to their objectives. Task Force Lovelady would capture more than sixteen 88mm guns at the local airport. The task forces under Colonel Leander Doan of CCA would have the honors of striking into the heart of the city. The task force would be spearheaded by a Pershing tank from Company E, 2nd Battalion, 32nd Armored Regiment commanded by Sergeant Robert Early. A few tanks of the German 106th Panzer Brigade were all that stood between the Americans and the Rhine. The famous tank duel between a German Panther and the Pershing would be caught on dramatic film by signal corps' cameramen Leon Rosenmann and James Bates. Again, please see the book *Spearhead* by Adam Makos for the incredible detailed story of this event. Cologne was cleared by the end of the day on the 6th and the 3rd Armored enjoyed their prize by exploring the city and liberating its stock of liquor and wine. By 17 March, the 104th Infantry Division replaced the 3rd Armored and a short period of rest and refitting was once again in order. The next target was even bigger than Cologne: it was the industrial heart of Germany, the Ruhr. The 3rd Armored would be given a critical role in closing the Ruhr pocket and then into the heartland of Germany. The division was sent to the north-east of Bonn for their brief period of rest.

The division launched their next attack on 23 March and moved across the Rhine into central Germany. The German 11th Panzer Division among other tattered army units attempted to stem the tide, but the armored spearhead could not be stopped. They fought near Altenkirchen where resistance did prove tough, but the 3rd Armored quickly overcame the defense. The Rivers Dill and Sieg were taken, along with the towns of Dillenburg, Herborn and then Marburg. The 104th Infantry Division had units attached to the 3rd Armored at this time to fill out the armored and infantry task forces. Pockets of surrendering German troops were being encountered faster than the division could process them, so the armored units would race forward while rear corps units would deal with the PoW processing. The advance was swift and monumental and Major General Rose was never prouder of his unit. The order then came for the division to swing north towards Paderborn to close the pocket and meet up with the 2nd Armored who were doing the same from their area in the north. It was here at Paderborn that the 3rd Armored would lose their beloved commander and be rudely reminded that the German Army did have some fight left in it after all.

The division turned to the north after receiving their orders on 28 March. Paderborn was called the Fort Knox of Germany, home to a German tank school and base for replacement and training troops. An ad hoc German battle group, SS Brigade Westfalen had been formed around a heavy Tiger tank battalion, the s.Pz.Abt 507 and a few armored Waffen SS replacement and training battalions. The cadre was mostly younger soldiers but the leadership was men with experience from the Western and Eastern Fronts. Task Force Hogan was given the area around Wewer, while the task forces of Lovelady, Welborn, Richardson and Miller (Doan) would head straight up the gut to Paderborn. Task Force Richardson peeled off into Kirchborchen and Nordborchen on 30 March and the town was quickly given the name 'bazooka town' by the Americans as one company lost more than eight medium tanks. German panzerfaust teams wreaked havoc on the attackers and it wasn't until the Americans brought flame-throwers into the battle did they gain control of the town. Task Force Lovelady was following Welborn on the advance and was engaging tough pockets of resistance around towns like Wrexen and Scherfede. Task Force Welborn made its way through Obermarsberg and through Etteln before moving towards Schloss Hamborn on the evening of the 30th. It was here that his column was cut in half by Tiger II tanks of the German battle group. The tanks moved up and down the column destroying tanks and half-tracks at will. Among those cut off was the column of Major General Rose who was following Welborn's troops. Confusion ensued and in the attempt to reach safety, Rose and his men found themselves surrounded by German Tiger tanks. A full investigation was conducted into the death of Major General Rose, but the consensus is that a trigger-happy German tank commander shot him as he was attempting to surrender and loosen his holster. News quickly spread about the death and the division was heartbroken but also angry. Brigadier General Doyle Hickey took over command of the division after the death of Rose. The next day three of the German Tiger II tanks were knocked out near the Schloss Hamborn and the division continued on their advance to Paderborn. Near the railyard and airport, the task forces of the 32nd Armored Regiment pushed out the stubborn

German defenders and the city was taken on 1 April. The next day elements of Task Force Kane of the 32nd Armored Regiment met up with the 2nd Armored Division at Lippstadt, essentially closing the Ruhr Pocket, which in memory of Major General Maurice Rose was now named the Rose Pocket.

The war in Europe would be over in a little over a month with the 3rd Armored Division pulled off the line by 25 April, but there were still some towns to take, rivers to cross and, unbeknown to the division, a concentration camp to be liberated. The next major obstacle for the division was the River Weser where they needed to cross to help seal off any escape routes of the German troops in the Harz Mountain area. Once again the name of the game was towns with the occasional log roadblocks, hidden panzerfaust teams and the random German Tiger tank that would pop up and cause havoc. A brief battle at Carlshafen on the convergence of the Rivers Diemel and Weser on 7 April resulted in more than ten tanks being lost by Task Force Welborn. Men of the division would cross the Weser at Gieselwerder and Beverungen and battle tanks at Harste, Ottbergen and near Osterode. On 10 April, the 83rd Armored Reconnaissance Battalion discovered a V-2 rocket facility outside Dora and Nordhausen. The next day further discovery was made of a concentration camp at Nordhausen where men of the division were pressed into duty to care for the liberated camp survivors. The River Saale was crossed on 13 April, while CCA battled near Sangerhausen. The war was dwindling, but short bitter battles took place at the Köthen airfield, Task Force Richardson at Bobbau-Steinfurth and in Thurland where the command post of Task Force Lovelady was overrun by a small German battle group and elements of the 83rd Reconnaissance Battalion came to their rescue. This very unit lost their beloved commander, Lieutenant Prentiss Yeomans on 18 April near Dessau when he was killed in action. The division moved to the River Mulde and Elbe areas at the Dessau area where the final battles of the unit would take place. The men that died in and around Dessau would be the last casualties for the division as they would be pulled out of the line and replaced by their familiar friends of the 9th Infantry Division.

From the beaches of Normandy to Dessau and the River Elbe with a detour back to Belgium for the Battle of the Bulge, the men of the 3rd Armored fought in every major engagement of the ETO. As their nickname stated, they were in fact the 'Spearhead' of the American Army in the ETO. General George Patton and his Third Army got all the press, but it was the 3rd Armored that led the way through France, Belgium, Germany, back to Belgium and then into the heartland of Germany. They lost thousands of soldiers including their beloved commander Maurice Rose, but the core of the unit, the veterans and their intensive training are what made the division successful in their mission. The war was over for the division and the men would begin to rotate home, taking their memories, both good and bad, back with them to the safety of the United States.

The 3rd Armored Division was in rest and refitting mode for about a month after the Ardennes offensive and moved back to the Stolberg area in early February. Here, men of Company I, 32nd Armored Regiment clean their tanks' treads on 8 February.

Tankers of the Assault Platoon, HQ Company, 2nd Battalion, 33rd Armored Regiment watch company artist T/5 John Garner draw a grim valentine for Hitler in Stolberg on 11 February.

On 22 February, First US Army Commander, General Courtney Hodges went to Gressenich, Germany to inspect the new M26 tank known as the 'Pershing'. The 3rd Armored received an initial allotment of ten of the tanks and they were issued between the two tank regiments. Major General Rose can be seen looking up at Hodges as he inspects the new tank.

Another view of General Hodges inspecting one of the new Pershing tanks in Gressenich. The tanks would do test-firing in this area as well and then see their first taste of combat by the end of the month.

Based on the registration number, this Pershing tank is from Company E, 32nd Armored Regiment: Sergeant Bob Early's tank, featuring the gunner Clarence Smoyer made famous by the great book *Spearhead* by Adam Makos. This photo shows the Pershing in the midst of firing tests at Gressenich in February.

Another photo of a different Pershing in test-firing in the same area. This photo was taken from the Gray Report which documented the Zebra Mission which was the implementation of the Pershing tank in the ETO.

The 3rd Armored moved through the Düren bridgehead on 26 February for their assault past the River Roer towards Golzheim, Blatzheim and beyond. Here an M36 90mm GMC and an M3A1 half-track from the 23rd Armored Engineer Battalion prepare to move out in the initial advance. The half-track is named 'Achtung'.

An M36
90mm GMC
of Company
A, 703rd Tank
Destroyer
Battalion
attached to Task
Force Kane sits
mired in mud
outside the
village of Buir,
Germany on 26
February.

As mortar shells
rain down on
Golzheim,
medics from the
32nd Armored
Regiment carry
a wounded
infantryman
into a shelter
or possibly
the half-track
ambulance
behind them.
26 February
in Golzheim,
Germany.

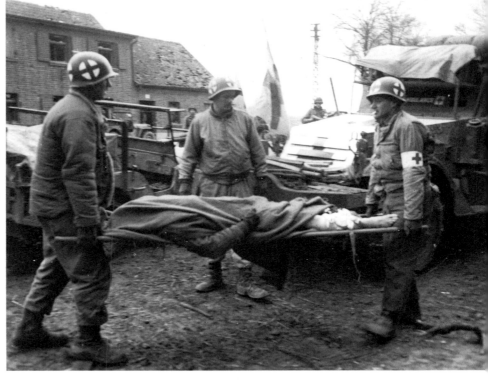

The German defense of Golzheim and Blatzheim was short-lived but spirited. Here a 3rd Armored Division half-track burns after receiving an artillery or mortar hit in Golzheim on 26 February.

A late-version StuG III Ausf.G sits knocked out in an embankment in the 3rd Armored Division sector on 26 February. The vehicle has a roof-mounted remote-control MG34 in front of the loader's hatch.

Smoke pours out of an M4A1 (76) medium tank just hit on the way to Bergerhausen, possibly near Blatzheim, making this tank possibly from Task Force Miller, 32nd Armored Regiment.

A photograph of the previous tank showing the aftermath of being hit and burning. The logs on the side were typical of the 3rd Armored at this time in the war.

A captured German 88mm artillery piece used in the defense around Blatzheim. This particular position using a Jagdpanther gun was facing south-west to Golzheim and another one was 300 yards to the north-west.

Another improvised Jagdpanther 88mm gun used as an anti-tank position typical of what the 3rd Armored encountered in this area of Germany across the Roer in late February 1945.

The Pershings of the 2nd Battalion, 32nd Armored Regiment saw their first action at Blatzheim on 26-27 February. After the battle, ordnance men took photographs to show the difference of track widths between the Pershing and M4 medium tanks.

Tanks of the 3rd Armored Division, including an M4A3E2 'Jumbo', move past the typical roadblock or 'Panzersperren' made of logs, encountered in German villages at this time in the war in the ETO. The vehicles are with Task Force Kane of the 32nd Armored Regiment.

Men of the 3rd Armored Division push a half-track through the mud near Mannheim. The soft ground on the Cologne plain was churned into mud by the advancing mechanized forces of the First Army. 27 February.

German prisoners are guarded in Blatzheim by soldiers of the 8th Infantry Division who were attached to the 3rd Armored Division. The log roadblock has been dismantled wide enough for columns of vehicles to pass through. 27 February.

A closer look at some of the German prisoners from the previous photo. Note the wide range of ages apparent here, from the old to quite young. These were typical of the units encountered by the 3rd Armored in the ETO during these final months of the war.

An M4A3 (76) HVSS from Task Force Richardson, 32nd Armored Regiment moves across a treadway bridge built by engineers over the Erft Canal near Paffendorf on 28 February.

Another tank crossing the same bridge as above, also an M4A3 (76) with a T20 turret and M1A1C gun with thread protector on the muzzle rather than a muzzle brake. Note the lucky horseshoe hanging by the pair of boots on the glacis plate driver's side.

Vehicles of the 33rd Armored Regiment gather in a town square in Angelsdorf on 28 February: a wide variety of vehicles including a jeep, a half-track, an M5A1 light tank and an M4 medium tank.

A military policeman from the 3rd Armored Division watches two civilians being interrogated by soldiers, probably from military intelligence. Note the 3rd Armored insignia on the soldier's helmet.

In Elsdorf on 26 February, 'Fireball', a T26E3 from Company F, 1st Battalion, 33rd Armored Regiment was knocked out by a Tiger 1 tank. The gunner and loader of the Pershing were killed. The tank would be repaired and returned to combat. Here a soldier points to one of the shell-holes.

Part of the Gray Report mentioned earlier contains the photos of 'Fireball' after it was knocked out so as to analyze why it was lost and record any lessons learned. The name can be seen on the side of the tank here.

Ordnance men inspect the damage done to 'Fireball' in Elsdorf. The shell-hole seen in the earlier photo is visible in this shot as well.

Here is the Tiger 1, number 201 of sPzAbt 301 that knocked out 'Fireball' the night before. After knocking out the Pershing, the Tiger backed up and became stuck in the debris on the street, was abandoned and captured by US troops the next day.

Sergeant Nick Mashlonik and his Pershing crew with Company E, Task Force Lovelady avenged 'Fireball' the next day on 27 February when they knocked out a Tiger 1, number 211 in Elsdorf and two Panzer IVs of the 9th Panzer Division on the outskirts.

Sergeant Mashlonik takes a closer look at one of his tank victims. Standing to his right is L.R. Slim Price, who was a civilian and gunnery expert from the States who was part of the Zebra Mission to observe the Pershing in action.

Panzer IV '223' of the 9th Panzer Division knocked out on 27 February by Sergeant Mashlonik and his crew near the railroad tracks leading from Elsdorf.

A different angle of the same tank from above showing the railroad track location where it was knocked out outside Elsdorf.

A third view of the same
tank from a little bit further
away. This photo was taken
by a maintenance officer
attached to Task Force
Lovelady.

This is the second Panzer IV knocked out by Sergeant Mashlonik outside Elsdorf on 27 February. Note the typical late-war camouflage foliage applied to German tanks at this stage.

Another photo taken by the Task Force Lovelady maintenance officer. Here is a Tiger 1 knocked out in a muddy field. No date or location, but given the limited details we know, it is probably from s.PzAbt 301 and was lost around the Elsdorf area in late February.

A closer view of the Tiger 1 shown above: visible now is the tank number '123' and also the damage done to the tank's 88mm cannon. The tank also has a coat of Zimmerit paste applied to it.

Glesch is next to Paffendorf and this German Panther tank from the 9th Panzer Division was captured by 3rd Armored Division and 4th Cavalry Group soldiers in early March. It is an Ausf.A Panther tank.

An M4A3 (76) medium tank of the 3rd Armored Division moves into Quadrath on 2 March. As the caption notes, flames from burning houses are still smoking in the background of this town across the Erft Canal. Soldiers from the 104th Infantry helped clear the town.

A pair of M5A1 light tanks of the 3rd Armored Division move past German civilians of Pulheim on their way to the prize city of Cologne on 4 March.

The 3rd Armored task force moves through Bergheim on the way to Cologne. A bulldozer works on clearing debris to ensure that the armored columns have a clear path on their advance.

Through the vantage of a shell-torn building overlooking a German cemetery, the signal corps' cameraman has photographed a half-track of the 3rd Armored Division moving through Pulheim on the way to Cologne.

M5A1 light tanks of the 2nd Battalion, 32nd Armored Regiment, Task Force X move off along the west side of the Cologne airfield on 5 March. The medium tank company went first, followed by the light tank company, looking south-east from Mengenich.

Tanks and infantry of the 3rd Armored Division move past a roadblock of trolley cars on the outskirts of Cologne.

Under an overpass in Cologne, troops of the 3rd Armored disassemble a roadblock while a tank from Company E, 32nd Armored Regiment moves through a narrow gap.

The other side of the previous image showing the jeeps of the 3rd Armored waiting to move once the trolley cars used as a roadblock were pulled out by tanks of the 32nd Armored Regiment.

On the left
is Colonel
Leander Doan,
commanding
officer of the
32nd Armored
Regiment, and
the other officer
is Lieutenant
Colonel William
Orr commanding
the 1st Battalion,
36th Armored
Infantry
Regiment. They
are planning the
advance into
Cologne.

On the outskirts of Cologne on 5 March, left to right: Colonel Leander Doan, Brigadier Doyle Hickey and CG Major General Maurice Rose.

Command group meeting in Cologne on 5 March. From left to right: Major Owenton (XO of the 36th AIR), Lieutenant Colonel William Orr, Colonel Leander Doan, Lieutenant Colonel William Miller (2nd Battalion, 32nd Armored) and Captain H.C. Morgan, Liaison Officer, 67th Armored Field Artillery Battalion.

M4 medium tanks from the 32nd Armored Regiment roll down a street in Cologne towards the famous cathedral. To the right is a civilian car that was hit by tank fire during the battle between the column and German tanks.

Another view of 3rd Armored Division tanks moving towards the Cologne cathedral, the site of the famous Pershing and Panther tank duel.

An M4 medium tank moves past the debris on the Cologne streets towards the cathedral.

A view of the famous Pershing of Cologne as it stands guard near the cathedral. Note the unit's markings on the fender and also the registration number on the front of the tank.

An M4A3 medium tank and, based on the markings, a tank assigned to the 32nd Armored Regiment headquarters moves past a destroyed trolley car in downtown Cologne.

By 6 March the fighting in Cologne had stopped and the 3rd Armored could rest. Here an M4A3E2 assault tank moves through the ruins on patrol. This tank was one of approximately 100 that had been upgraded with a 76mm gun earlier in the year.

Action shot of the Pershing and Panther duel that shows the Panther receiving direct hits from the Pershing of Sergeant Robert Early and his gunner Clarence Smoyer.

After the duel, the Panther at the cathedral was a magnet for photos. Here, two of the Pershing crew, Homer Davis and John DeRiggi, check out their latest victim.

Photo of the Panther taken shortly
after it was hit, as is evident from
the smoke still coming from the
burning vehicle.

The partner of signal corps'
cameraman Harold Roberts was
Clarence Garrell who primarily took
motion pictures for the camera team.
Here is a photo of Garrell in front of
the Cologne cathedral Panther tank.

Defending the outskirts of Cologne was a ring of German 88mm gun emplacements that could be used in both the air and anti-armor role. Here is one of the destroyed gun emplacements.

According to the official caption, the Germans destroyed this 88mm gun before retreating from the advancing Americans near Cologne.

M4 medium tanks of the 3rd Armored roll through Kerpen in support of the 8th Infantry Division on 16 March.

After taking Cologne, the 3rd Armored Division had about two weeks off to rest and refit before taking part in closing the Ruhr pocket. Here a soldier in a jeep poses in front of an M4 medium tank in Frechen in mid-March 1945.

During a break in the March 1945 action, Major General Lawton Collins of VII Corps awards Staff Sergeant Robert Fairchild, a tank platoon leader in the 33rd Armored Regiment, the Distinguished Service Cross for his actions in September at the Westwall.

Somewhere on the advance around the closing of the Ruhr pocket, these two M5A1 light tanks pass a German half-track being used in the medical role.

Exact date and location unknown, but this Jagdpanther was photographed by an officer with Task Force Lovelady sometime in the spring of 1945.

A knocked-out Panzer IV/70 (v) somewhere in the 3rd Armored Division sector in Germany, probably around the time the Ruhr pocket was being closed.

Who said the American GI didn't have a sense of humor? This German Panzer IV/70(V) fell victim to the 3rd Armored Division and the men of Spearhead wanted everyone to know the facts.

Two Panzer IV/70 (V) from the 3rd Panzergrenadier Division that were knocked out by the 3rd Armored Division lay near Oberpleis on 25 March.

Close-up photo of tank E11 of the 33rd Armored Regiment that took an armor-piercing shot almost directly under the assistant driver/bow gunner's position. This photo was taken in March 1945.

Another Company E medium tank of the 33rd Armored Regiment in the spring of 1945. This tank, an M4A3 (75) numbered E15, has been fitted with extra armor-plating on the front for added protection against panzerfausts and other armor-piercing weapons.

The T26E3 Pershing tank of Sergeant Nicholas Mashlonik moves through Altenkirchen on 27 March 1945. This particular Pershing has been upgraded with cement on the front for extra protection since it was photographed in February.

An M5A1 light tank with GIs hitching a ride follows the Pershing through Altenkirchen.

A 3rd Armored soldier directs tank traffic down the same street in Altenkirchen. The next tank in line is an M4A3E2 assault tank or 'Jumbo'. These vehicles are with Task Force Lovelady of the 33rd Armored Regiment.

An M4A1 (76) with a thick piece of armor added to the front makes its way through Altenkirchen on 27 March. This tank has the hatch configuration seen on earlier 33rd Armored Regiment tanks with the loader's and commander's hatches swapped.

An M7 105mm HMC rolls past GIs of the 104th Infantry Division and some German nurses in Eichelhardt on 27 March. The 104th had some units attached to the 3rd Armored Division at this time, with the rest of the division working in the same area of operations.

Tanks and vehicles of the 3rd Armored Division with 104th Infantry GIs aboard moved through Altenkirchen on 27 March. The tank has an extra plate of armor and in the distance to the left, the signal corps' cameraman who filmed the motion picture footage of this advance can be seen.

An M4A3 medium tank of Company F, 33rd Armored Regiment waits for orders to advance in the vicinity of Rettersen and Hasselbach on 26 March. There is a tank in the background moving through a cloud of smoke.

MPs of the 3rd Armored Division check German prisoners of war captured in Rettersen and Hasselbach on 26 March.

An M4 medium tank of the 3rd Armored Division passes a destroyed Panzer IV near Bad Marienberg on 28 March 1945. The 3rd Armored Division was about to swing north and close the Ruhr pocket.

An M4 medium tank of the Spearhead advances past a German medical vehicle and discarded equipment on the roadside on their advance to Herborn during the rapid advance on 28 March.

An M4A1 (76) with an extra plate of armor added to the front for protection moves through a town in the Obermarsberg area in their advance to the Paderborn area on 30 March 1945. This tank belongs to Task Force Welborn which on the next day would be ambushed by Tiger II tanks around Paderborn.

A view of the same street as above as tanks and half-tracks roll through the town on the way to Paderborn. Curious German civilians line the street to watch the Americans. The town is most likely either Husen, Henglarn or Amt Attlen.

An M5A1 light tank from the headquarters unit of the 33rd Armored Regiment inspects a German vehicle on a wooded rail on the advance to Paderborn, 30 March 1945.

The advance towards Paderborn was a lightning one. Here an M5A1 light tank moves past a fire near some buildings on the way to Paderborn on 30 March.

German prisoners stand in a farmyard guarded by a few 3rd Armored Division soldiers. They are awaiting trucks to take them back to the rear. This photo was taken on 30 March during the advance of Task Force Welborn to Paderborn.

After clearing the town of Henglarn, Task Force Welborn moved towards Etteln on 30 March. On the outskirts they encountered several pockets of resistance consisting of Waffen SS troops, many of them teenagers. Here half-tracks flush out snipers from a hillside spot.

Photo from the same area outside Etteln. A group of 3rd Armored soldiers fire at enemy troops from their half-track. The vehicle is from the 2nd Battalion of the 36th Armored Infantry Regiment which was part of Task Force Welborn.

A group of young German soldiers carry a wounded comrade back to the rear lines of the 3rd Armored past a half-track of the 36th Armored Infantry Regiment.

A medic with the 3rd Armored helps a wounded German soldier from the SS Brigade Westfalen down a hill to the American lines.

An M8 Armored Reconnaissance Car named 'Roaring Estelle' with the 33rd Armored Reconnaissance Company fires on snipers in the vicinity of Etteln on 30 March.

A still from signal corps' motion picture footage from the same area and action of the previous photos outside Etteln on 30 March. Here an M4 (105) assault gun of Task Force Welborn has deployed off the main road after engaging the enemy.

An M31 Armored Recovery Vehicle of Task Force Welborn at the foot of the hill seen in the photo on page 279 before this in which the German SS troopers were being flushed out.

An M4A3 (105) assault gun moves past a field strewn with German medical vehicles in Lixfeld on 29 March. The vehicle the tank is about to pass is a Dodge 4x4 ¾-ton Command Reconnaissance Car.

An M5A1 light tank passes a burning building in Ludwigshütte on 29 March during the rapid advance in closing the Ruhr pocket.

Soldiers take cover behind their jeep while a medic tends to their comrade in a ditch off the road near Korbach on 30 March.

The same area as the previous photo and this is the tank seen in the background. Smoke blows in the distance as 3rd Armored soldiers return fire into Korbach before moving further into the town.

An M4A1 (76) crew moves out of their tank while engaging German units around Korbach. This photo is presumably taken in the same area as the previous two. The tank has a large piece of armor added to the glacis for extra protection and the commander's hatch is a split-hatch rather than the all-round-vision cupola.

A common scene in the ETO during the spring of 1945. A rapid armored column advances past burning buildings. Here an M5a1 moves past a burning building in Frankenberg on 30 March.

A photo from the Gray Report which was documenting the T26E3 Pershing in combat in the ETO. Here a Pershing attached to the 3rd Armored Division undergoes maintenance work on its engine.

An M4A3E2 assault tank that has been fitted with a 76mm gun somewhere in Germany in March or April 1945.

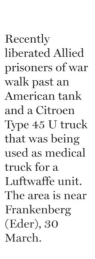

Recently liberated Allied prisoners of war walk past an American tank and a Citroen Type 45 U truck that was being used as medical truck for a Luftwaffe unit. The area is near Frankenberg (Eder), 30 March.

Also near Frankenberg is an m.Zgkw. (8-ton) Sd.Kfz.7 fitted with a crane and that may have been in the process of pulling the Sd.Kfz 10/4 or 10/5 behind it when it was knocked out.

An M3 Scout Car moves over a treadway pontoon bridge over the River Weser in early April. The photo was taken from the remnants of a bridge that had been blown by the retreating Germans.

An M3A1 half-track of the 83rd Armored Reconnaissance Battalion somewhere in Germany around March/April. The vehicle is named 'Hey Louise' and features some female silhouettes on the door. (© *George H. Bloth Collection*)

Infantrymen, including one with a radio, hitch a ride on an M4A3 HVSS (76) somewhere in Germany in April 1945. The road conditions appear to be very sloppy. (© *George H. Bloth Collection*)

Taken at the exact same spot as the above photo, an M4A3E2 assault tank, upgraded to a 76mm gun and loaded down with GIs makes its way down the muddy road. There appears to be something of interest to the two men in the front as they peer down the road. (© *George H. Bloth Collection*)

Typical 3rd Armored Division tankers in late 1945 in Germany. A crew of an M5A1 light tank with a cowgirl logo painted on the side poses for the cameraman during their advance. (© *George H. Bloth Collection*)

Another M3A1 half-track of the 83rd Armored Reconnaissance Battalion. This one is named 'Harry James' and has markings on the front bumper indicating it is from the maintenance unit of the 83rd. (© George H. Bloth Collection)

An M3A1 half-track of the 67th Armored Field Artillery Battalion moving through a German village in the spring of 1945.

The crew of an M7 105mm HMC checks out their vehicle's tracks outside Ringleben, Germany. The vehicle is from the 67th Armored Field Artillery Battalion.

Probably one of the last photos of Major General Maurice Rose taken before his death on 31 March. This photograph was taken on 24 March at the Maurer Estate near Remagen and the division was receiving a Presidential Unit Citation and Rose himself a Bronze Star from VII Corps Commander Lawton Collins and First Army Commander Courtney Hodges to his right.

Vehicles of the 3rd Armored cross a pontoon bridge over the River Weser on 9 April at Beverungen. The 3rd Armored was driving deeper into Germany every day, sealing the southern escape routes from the Harz Mountains for the German forces there.

Troops of the 3rd Armored Division with a mix of jeeps and medium tanks rest in the April sunshine after moving into the town of Geselwerder.

A German train with 128mm flak guns on board lays smoldering after an artillery barrage by the 3rd Armored Division near Lenglern, Germany on 9 April by CCB.

This photo was taken on 10 April in Carlshafen just a few days after Task Force Welborn lost eleven tanks, one on the opposite side of the Weser. The US tanks column was hemmed in by German 200 kilogram cratering charges across from the bridge. Once six tanks had passed, they blew the charges, resulting in the stopped column ran into charges laid across the road near the bridge. Then from across the river a German anti-tank gun picked off the tanks. In this photo, engineers walk past four of those tanks, three medium and one light.

An M4 medium tank loaded down with GIs moves past an MP motorcycle and two M36 90mm gun motor carriages outside the village of Hardegsen on 10 April.

An M3A1 half-track of the 3rd Armored Division moves past a field with German farmers that seem oblivious to the rapid advance of the American Army. This area was near Duderstadt, 10 April. The vehicle has markings of the 23rd Armored Engineer Battalion.

Another M3A1 half-track loaded down with 3rd Armored soldiers makes its way down a German highway with farmland on either side. This open country was a welcome change from the tight hedgerows of France that first greeted the unit when they reached the ETO.

Trucks and an M3A1 half-track of the 3rd Armored cross the River Saale over a treadway pontoon bridge in April 1945. The engineers were building bridges as needed at a furiously quick pace.

An M4A1 Mortar Carrier of the 3rd Armored Division troops outside Werben and Stumsdorf on 14 April. It has been modified by reversing the sides of the rear compartment so that the ammunition stowage was at the rear, allowing the mortar to be fired over the cab. Note the dust circles that have formed around the door of the ammunition rack.

The town burning in the background is Stumsdorf on 14 April as tanks of the 3rd Armored move into the newly-liberated town.

With smoke billowing in the distance, a 3rd Armored Division unit has deployed into a field with trucks and half-tracks. Closest to the camera is an M3A1 half-track with a trailer attached to its rear.

Outside Bobbau-Steinfurth on around 18 April are two German Jagdpanzer 38s. Task Force Richardson attacked this area and was met with an enemy tank and infantry force counter-attack. This attack was quickly turned back by heavy artillery and air-cooperation fighter-bombers, which accounted for eight enemy tanks.

One of the new M24 'Chaffee' light tanks that the 83rd Armored Reconnaissance Battalion received in the spring of 1945. Here this M24 guards a crossroads in Sangerhausen.

A great side view of an M24 light tank of the 83rd Armored Reconnaissance Battalion in a German village in April 1945. While they entered the war at a late stage, they were still a welcome upgrade on the M5A1 light tank. (© *George H. Bloth Collection*)

M36 90mm tank destroyers of the 703rd Tank Destroyer Battalion and half-tracks of the 36th Armored Infantry Regiment deploy off the road near Dessau on 17 April. Based on the markings of the half-track, it is from Company G, 3rd Battalion, making this part of Task Force Richardson, 32nd Armored Regiment.

A lone jeep of the 3rd Armored enters Thurland on 18 April. According to the caption, the town was under a German artillery barrage at the time. The driver of the jeep is wearing an Army Air Force bomber jacket.

An M5A1 light tank 'Africa' from Company A of either the 32nd or 33rd Armored Regiment fires with their machine gun into the woods outside Dessau.

After receiving an armor-piercing shell hit on the tracks of their M3A1 half-track, men of the 36th Armored Infantry Regiment work on removing a wheel from the bogie assembly outside Thurland on 18 April.

Airplane mechanics work on the engine of a Piper L-4 'Grasshopper' in a field outside Thurland on 18 April. Another plane sits in the background. These planes were critical in the observation role for artillery units of the 3rd Armored Division.

T/4 Weslyn Sucher of Oshkosh, WI stands in front of an M8 75mm Howitzer Motor Carriage outside Dessau on 17 April. Sucher was part of the 83rd Armored Reconnaissance Battalion.

The next five photos show men and vehicles of the 67th Armored Field Artillery Battalion at the end of the war. Here two soldiers stand in front of their M7 105mm howitzer motor carriage.

The same two soldiers from the previous photograph are now standing near an M31 Armored Recovery Vehicle with a half-track in the background.

'Sunny South', an M3A1 half-track of the Service Company of the 67th Armored Field Artillery Battalion. A tarp has been placed over the rear of the vehicle and the .50 caliber machine gun.

The same tank as pictured previously, now showing a close-up view of the extra armor that has been added to the front glacis. Another M4 medium tank sits to the left.

A GI of the 67th Armored Field Artillery Battalion sits on the front of a Field Observer's M4A3 (75) medium tank from the Headquarters Company of the battalion. Extra armor has been added to the front glacis.